BANFF AND BUCHAN

**This book is to be ret..... .efore
the last date stan.... below.**

In Pursuit of Quality

IN PURSUIT
OF QUALITY

The Case Against
ISO 9000

John Seddon

Oak Tree Press
Dublin • London

Oak Tree Press
Merrion Building
Lower Merrion Street
Dublin 2, Ireland

4 Alexandra Road
Twickenham,
Middlesex TW1 2HE
United Kingdom

A catalogue record of this book is
available from the British Library.

ISBN 1-86076-042-2↑

Printed in the Republic of Ireland by Colour Books Ltd.

CONTENTS

PREFACE

It has been generally assumed that ISO 9000 registration makes a positive contribution to quality and competitive performance. The purpose of this book is to offer a different view. We shall set out the evidence and argue the case against ISO 9000 as a contribution to quality, productivity and competitive position. In simple terms, we shall argue that ISO 9000 makes you worse off, not better off. Our hope is that in taking an antagonistic position, we will provide a spur to managers who have little or insufficient knowledge of quality or who perhaps have developed indifference. Too many managers express the cynical view that quality is only concerned with "plaques and flags", an understandable view given what they have experienced.

ISO 9000 is a quality management standard supposedly aimed at improving economic performance. Our whole system is driven towards the adoption of ISO 9000. Government organisations and many of the larger private sector organisations insist that their suppliers register as a prerequisite for tendering. In the UK, Training and Enterprise Councils (TECs) are measured on their ability to persuade organisations to register to it, and the Standard itself encourages organisations to impose a requirement on their suppliers to register. Today there are more than 52,000 UK businesses registered to ISO 9000, and about the same number of businesses registered throughout the rest of the world.

Since 1979 the British Government has taken an active role in ISO 9000's promulgation and today ISO 9000 has its own institutions: there are committees responsible for re-writing it and a multi-layered bureaucracy which licenses service organisations to live off the proceeds of assessing organisations against it. There are a plethora of training courses and armies of advisers and consultants, many of whom, armed with less than a week's training, sally forth as "experts" and impose their understanding of the Standard on unsuspecting managers who, on the one hand, feel obliged to follow suit and, on the other, hope only to improve their organisations.

Quality first came to the notice of business managers more than 50 years ago. It is still the most important and least understood subject on the management curriculum. Innovation and competitive position rely on being better, smarter and cheaper; quality thinking provides a method. Improving quality always results in greater productivity; improved productivity leads to lower prices and greater market-share. Quality provides the means to greater prosperity and a more secure future for organisations and their employees. But does ISO 9000 make a contribution in this regard? Our answer is an unequivocal *no*. This book has been written to put a spoke in the wheel of a phenomenon we have come to regard as seriously dysfunctional.

If the Standard and its institutions exist to make a positive contribution, it follows that a critical examination of their achievement can, ultimately, only improve what we are setting out to do. To develop our arguments against ISO 9000, we shall explore the Standard, what people do with it and what they might have done if they had taken a different view of the circumstances they faced.

By being labelled a quality Standard, ISO 9000 has only succeeded in steering quality into troubled waters. Far from being a first step to quality, it has been a step in the wrong direction. The hope is that it hasn't conditioned management to lose interest in the subject. If it has, it is only a matter of time before an economic jolt will wake them up. We don't want to wait until it's too late. We think the best way to regain management's attention is to be honest about the failure of ISO 9000. After all, there is a better way.

ACKNOWLEDGEMENTS

This book has been written in collaboration with Richard Davis, Ibrar Hussain, Matt Loughran and Barry Wrighton. We are a group within the Vanguard consulting organisation who share deep concerns about what we have seen happening in organisations as a consequence of ISO 9000. We are indebted to Carolyn Brice, Ted Clarke, Brent Gathercole, David Givens, Ian Graham, Neil Martin, Gary Purser, Val Thomas, Chris Whitfield, Joyce Wilson, and Dave Young, all of whom gave up their time to read the first manuscript and provide feedback.

A special note of thanks to my daughter Jodie who brought fresh eyes and an intelligent mind to the final editing. If she can be persuaded, starting from a position of knowing nothing about ISO 9000, one would hope that those who purport to "know" can be encouraged to think again.

The reader will notice references to the work of W. Edwards Deming, who taught quality in Japan in the 1950s. He gained international recognition for his work much later in his life and much of what he taught still remains unfamiliar to most managers. We found his teachings inspiring. It was Deming's work which first showed us the importance of understanding the organisation as a system. This helped us understand why so many popular programmes of change had failed. It is from this perspective which we criticise ISO 9000. We hope that the reader will feel compelled to learn more about what he taught. Recommended reading is provided at the end of the book.

However, the responsibility for what is written here, as many authors say, lies with me. If a deep sense of despair and frustration shows through it is mine. There have been times when I could gladly have throttled those who in my worst moments I describe as anal cardigan-wearing types, for they have wrought havoc in our organisations and have presumed to label it as quality. I want to acknowledge responsibility for a human weakness: my passion can spill over. To those I have offended during the many debates, I apologise with sincerity. We must keep the debate going and, more importantly, involve managers in it. If we do, quality will win and if quality wins, we all win.

John Seddon
April 1997

Chapter 1

TEN ARGUMENTS AGAINST ISO 9000

It was 1986. On a Friday morning in May a newly appointed director of customer services found a file labelled "escalation" in his in-tray. He asked his secretary what it was. "These," she said, "are the customers who may ring you next week with a complaint. It is the escalation procedure, it started when we did BS 5750. It ensures you know what is going on."

He soon found out that the procedure began during a Wednesday morning meeting with field engineers reporting to their managers which customers were unhappy. These managers brought these reports to their superiors on Wednesday afternoons; the more senior group decided, during a meeting on Thursday mornings, which customers should go forward to the director's file. The director was furious. He issued an edict saying that in the future any customer who indicated unhappiness should be visited immediately by a manager who could understand the customer's problem and make a commitment to action. This, he insisted, should be the new procedure.

Next, the director called his assessor — the person from an organisation "accredited" with the competence to audit against BS 5750. He was told that the assessor's job was to assess the organisation as written in the physical documentation (manuals). If the procedures were judged as inappropriate by management, they could be changed and, if so, managers should remember to amend the documentation. (We visited this assessor seven years later. He had been closely involved with the early work on BS 5750 but now he was no longer an assessor. He told us that, in his view, BS 5750 had been the biggest confidence trick ever perpetrated on British industry. It is easy to have sympathy with his view.)

This "escalation procedure" was our first experience of BS 5750 (which later became ISO 9000). We had spent two years studying the failure of quality programmes (usually training courses — none up to that time related to BS 5750) and had become fascinated by the teachings of Deming. From what we had learned about quality, BS 5750 did not appear to make sense. The Standard bore no relation to what we had been learning.

We were persuaded to attribute the problem to inappropriate management thinking. The fault, it was argued, lay with over-emphasis on bureaucracy and internal control. The argument was (and still is) "BS 5750/ISO 9000 is OK if you do it right". We now know that we should have questioned it, but this was new to us and it had the backing of institutions. It was also hard to criticise something which was so difficult to understand. Furthermore, we were dissuaded from being critical, as criticism was received as an indication that you were not a supporter of the quality movement.

Through the 1980s and into the 1990s the bandwagon rolled on. Marketplace obligation, even coercion, meant an ever-increasing number of registrations to BS 5750/ISO 9000. We have witnessed a plethora of companies registering and failing to achieve the promised result — improvements in customer satisfaction, efficiency and other measures of performance.

As we shall demonstrate, the evidence suggests that registration to ISO 9000 is a guarantee of sub-optimal performance. In simple terms registration to ISO 9000 makes performance worse. It adds to costs, makes customers unhappy, demoralises staff; but most of all it prevents organisations taking opportunities to improve performance which they might otherwise have seen, "blinding" the means for improvement.

In every case we have studied we have found new activity, put in place because of ISO 9000 registration, making performance worse. More importantly, in every case we have seen how organisations have missed major opportunities for improvement. The Standard has encouraged these organisations to take a perspective on their world from which it is difficult, if not impossible, to take action to improve performance.

We will present many practical examples throughout the book in order to illustrate that, as the defenders argue, it is not just bad management or bad consulting advice which is at fault, although both have played their part. Our argument is that the Standard itself encourages managers to act on their organisations in ways which undermine performance. In all, a collection of influences — current managerial thinking, consultants' advice and the thinking implicit in the Standard, fuelled by the obligation to register — have led to ubiquitous damage to economic and competitive position. It is possible, and we would argue predictable, that ISO 9000 has inflicted damage to the competitive position of thousands of organisations. It is all the more disturbing that this should have occurred in the name of quality.

We will examine what ISO 9000 sets out to do (in chapter 2) and explore whether this is quality (throughout the book and, in particular, in chapters 4 and 6). We will argue that quality is defined in the mind of the customer, which leads us to the first argument in the case against ISO 9000:

1. ISO 9000 encourages organisations to act in ways which make things worse for their customers.

Recently, we called our telephone service provider with two simple requests. The service agent who took the call said she could action one of the requests but not the other as it fell into a different category (one request was classi-

fied as a service call, the other as maintenance). This seemed silly to us: these were both quite straightforward matters which could easily have been noted for action by anyone. It was, we were told, because of ISO 9000. Clearly managers or advisers had interpreted the Standard in such a way as to make service more difficult for the customer. The organisation lost: we didn't take either service.

Were we supposed to be grateful to be given another number to ring? How often do organisations registered to ISO 9000 make customers run an "organisational maze" to get service (and pay them for it)?

Our printer announced that he could no longer supply us with quotations over the telephone. He had become registered to ISO 9000 and this meant that paperwork had to go between us. Even using the fax we found that quotations now took at least four days. We changed printers.

The printer argued he was now a better quality company. We (his customer) thought his quality was worse.

One of the largest business-to-business printers in the UK was the first in its sector to register to ISO 9000. Five years on, because they were losing market-share, they undertook an exercise in finding out what mattered to their customers. What they found surprised them. Customers wanted faster quotations and were buying from competitors because the competitors were able to give quotes in two days (compared to their average of ten). They reorganised the quotations department and processes. They got the quotations time down to a day and, the last we heard, they were aiming at getting it down to minutes by pricing and negotiating with customers over the telephone.

Stories like this lead the defenders to argue that the managers could have done the "right" things as part of their registration to ISO 9000. But the fact of the matter is they did not. What they did instead is something which is of vital interest. What happens in practice should help us to ask questions which would lead to a better understanding of the Standard and quality (and whether the two are the same). Instead of doing what could have been done, these organisations, like many others, did things which made performance worse. It was of little value to the organisation above to have a well-documented and audited quotations procedure which was killing off their business. There are countless examples where an "internal focus" has led to worse performance, but in this case it was not just internally focused bureaucracy which was doing damage:

> *The quality co-ordinator had developed concerns about the Standard. In the drive for greater flexibility they had given more control of the work to the printing profession-als and no longer wanted others (quality controllers) to check their work. The quality manager had learned that checking increased errors. However, she was unable to convince her assessor that this was "good quality" (acceptable to his interpretation of the Standard). It re-sulted in record-keeping to serve the needs of the assessor and unnecessary "drudgery" as perceived by the print workers.*

Records enable the inspector to do his or her job. The require-ments for documentation are a major feature of the Standard: they represent the Standard's view of how one should go about checking whether organisations do as they say they do. The means for improvement lie elsewhere, but the documented sys-tem becomes the means for organisational control. Inspection means independent control of work, the "philosophy" of the Standard is grounded in "quality by inspection", but:

2. Quality by inspection is not quality.

This is our second argument in the case against ISO 9000. Inspection increases errors, adds to costs and decreases morale.

A Loss Adjuster was promoted to work in a larger branch. In her previous branch she had responsibility for her own work; in practical terms she signed everything she sent out. The branch manager in her new branch insisted that he signed all outgoing reports and typically he made changes according to his view of what constituted "good work". Within months the Loss Adjuster felt the quality of her work decline. She knew the branch manager would make changes according to his preferences and would, therefore, not take as much responsibility for ensuring the work was correctly completed. She knew the quality of her work was declining and she experienced a drop in morale, but she felt she could do nothing about it.

In such circumstances one often finds that the "inspecting" person does not inspect everything, assuming that the "worker" will have taken responsibility. Both parties are caught up in the psychology of inspection — each prone to assuming that the other will be responsible. It is a recipe for increasing errors. Many people have begun to have doubts about the value of ISO 9000's requirements for external and internal inspections: both controls are associated with bureaucracy, and many people rightly question whether this represents "quality" thinking.

The joke in the transport cafés is that Eddie Stobart doesn't have ISO 9000. His drivers laugh while others talk about having to do their "second job" — having done the work, they have to write about it; they have to fill in forms for the records required by the quality procedures. When we learned of this, we called Eddie Stobart. He too was subjected to "marketplace" coercion. People told him he might lose business if he did not register. But he had always felt that he ran a quality business and had good systems, and he distrusted the bandwagon which was surrounding ISO 9000, so he dug his heels in. He lost no business. There are others now who feel they might have been better off to have avoided the quality bandwagon.

There is very little research on the consequences of avoiding registration to ISO 9000, but the little there is shows that organisations have not suffered adversely, as many would predict. The emergence of doubts about the value of ISO 9000 has resulted in managers shopping around for assessors, wanting to find the assessor that will do the least damage. As long ago as the late 1980s assessing organisations were hearing their customers express serious discontent with ISO 9000 registration. These organisations have responded belatedly by changing the role definition of their "visiting professionals" from "assessing" to "auditing". They argue that the latter suggests they are in the business of providing advice and guidance — it has been driven by a recognition that they need to create value for their customers.

The original role, that of assessment, was the reason for the Standard's origins. The assessor was just that, someone who could relieve the first party (the customer) of the need to check on suppliers (it was assumed that checking could not be entrusted to the supplier). Now, it seems, the role of the assessor has been blurred: the auditor is both poacher and gamekeeper — to what extent might this result in advice being tailored to meet the needs of the paymaster? Is this new role getting us any closer to improving quality and competitive position, or does it run the risk of taking us further away? There is, quite naturally (because the system encourages it), evidence of abuse of the power of the auditor's role, which we discuss in chapter 7.

It was, in any event, assessors and their organisations who provided much of the guidance on the Standard's requirements. So to help us understand what has happened it is important to understand who the assessors are and, by implication, what knowledge they bring. A correspondent whose career spanned the introduction of quality standards talked of his experience of the early period of what was then BS 5750:

> *"The greatest fear we all had was where the 'assessors' would come from. We knew in our hearts that it would be from the redundant government inspectors and 'surplus' industry 'quality' managers. This has turned out to be the most disastrous part of the whole scheme. There are many ISO 9000 consultants I knew from their old industry days that frankly I wouldn't have around, and now I find them pontificating on how to run a business!"*

In the late 1980s Tom Peters (business guru and best-selling author) was alleged to have observed that "quality in the UK has been taken over by the 'procedures merchants'". He struck a chord with many. Now ISO 9000 is spreading to his home country (the USA) as well as many others. Yet there is no evidence to suggest that it has a beneficial effect on quality and economic performance.

Among British managers there is now wide acceptance of the view that registration to ISO 9000 is bad news (if you doubt this, talk about ISO 9000 at parties). Surely the mention of a quality Standard should produce a positive, energetic response — after all, quality is all about delighting the customer and we all want more of that, don't we?

Managers groan when ISO 9000 is mentioned because they know in their hearts that it is flawed. In the face of what they see in their organisations they know it doesn't feel right. They can point to unnecessary paperwork and bureaucracy, they relay the oft-cited view that you can deliver poor quality services and be registered to the Standard so long as you deliver according to the procedures you have laid down. They feel that this cannot be what quality is all about and they're right. ISO

9000 has a fundamentally flawed conception of quality. Rooted in the philosophy of quality by inspection, it encourages managers to control their organisations in ways which actually undermine performance and, paradoxically, damage quality. These methods of control are the reason behind people's dissatisfaction; they demoralise people. The methods of control are the focus for the third argument in the case against ISO 9000.

3. ISO 9000 starts from the flawed presumption that work is best controlled by specifying and controlling procedures.

This is why you find over-elaborate documentation, people having to do "two jobs" — do the work then "write" about it. In some cases you find documentation which only exists so that an external assessor can do his job! These methods are preventing people making a useful contribution, making them feel that the value of their contribution is, in whatever way, defined by procedures. Despite what many managers have been led to believe, to control performance by controlling people's activity is a poor way to manage. It is usually a fast way to sub-optimisation — it makes performance worse. (We return to this phenomenon and compare it with better methods of control in chapters 4 and 6.)

The following e-mail was sent to us by a government employee who was frustrated by the damage ISO 9000 had done to his organisation:

"Twelve months ago over 'two feet' of procedures arrived on my desk with the instructions that they were to be implemented immediately. Implementing those procedures increased our workload by, I would guess, 10 to 15 per cent. This was the start to ISO 9000.

We found that everything was beautifully detailed into sub-tasks for each procedure with a person responsible for each sub-task. But nobody was actually responsible for ensuring the overall activity was achieved. Innovation was totally stifled, the only way to do it was by the procedure. We had implemented some computerised bring-forward systems, more efficient but not in accordance with the procedures, so we had to go back to a manual paper system. Many procedures were written by people who didn't understand our jobs. In some cases the procedures were absurd in their impracticality.

Procedures were written on the basis of infinite time being available. Indeed threats have been made over the last year to work to procedure. There were so many of the damn things that nobody was ever sure if we were following all the correct procedures. If there was a task there was one or more procedures and signatures required at every point.

Twelve months later the amendments to the procedures are flying around at a furious rate to try and correct for the fact that people cannot (or, I have to admit in some cases, will not) follow all the procedures. The total cost of this exercise is circa £800,000 (excluding time spent learning procedures).

We got ISO 9000. Was it worth it? In my opinion, no. Talking to several major industrial companies, they will not implement ISO 9000 except where they are customer-facing and need it for PR purposes. Comments like "just a paper chase" are frequent. I work in a government department so the natural civil service way of working may have made things worse. The final straw today was a document which I am required to fill in yes/no. Unfortunately whoever revised the procedure had failed to actually add any questions.

Nice to see someone else admitting that the emperor has no clothes. Criticising 'quality' is like criticising the Queen Mum."

How many others experienced registration to ISO 9000 in this way? The question is extremely important if we are to prevent others doing the same, but it is not a question which is encouraged. The government believes ISO 9000 to be "a good thing". If this e-mail is representative of what has occurred in every government department, the costs (borne ultimately by taxpayers) are fantastic. Obvious costs, such as fees to auditors and consultants are significant, but the real costs are much larger — the costs of poor service, inefficiency and low morale become incalculable.

That organisations inflict such pain and suffering on themselves is itself an important phenomenon to understand. We believe it is inevitable when the principle reason for registration is coercion. Managers are fearful about what could happen if they are not registered. The focus of management activity becomes "get it". It is vital to them to avoid the consequences they fear in not having it. Management, when focused in this way, does not learn.

To take one example:

Computer engineers working in Scotland had the reputation of being the best in their company. Every year the Scottish team won the service and quality awards. The company had decided it had to get ISO 9000 for its maintenance division (Government customers were demanding it). The first the engineers knew about it was when a set of new work procedures arrived. On reading the procedures, the engineers sent a message to the centre to say the procedures were unworkable and, moreover, they would make performance worse. The project team responsible for ISO 9000 implementation (in the centre) logged the engineers' message. When we found it, four months had passed and no-one had been to listen to the engineers. The project team had been targeted with getting ISO 9000 by a certain date. Managers had decided what was important.

The managers and everybody involved with what they saw as a "project" ignored its implications for performance. They did not start with understanding performance, so how could they have hoped to improve it? They started instead with the desire to achieve registration to the Standard. They were encouraged to work this way because of the normal prescription for implementing ISO 9000, which is our fourth argument in the case against ISO 9000:

4. The typical method of implementation is bound to cause sub-optimisation of performance.

It does not start with performance, it starts with a view of the organisation compared to a set of requirements. It is of course assumed that the requirements will, when properly interpreted, have a beneficial impact on performance. But this is not proven, nor, we will argue, is it theoretically sound.

The focus of implementation is to create documentation which enables monitoring of the defined procedures. It is no surprise that organisations get into the position where they ignore the documented procedures until just prior to assessment — when there is an unholy rush to ensure everything is in order for the assessors. And the assessment is often a tortuous experience. As we shall see, much of the assessor's training focuses on "catching people doing things wrong". People do not like to be "caught out" or controlled, they like to be in control. To be told that a third party is the judge of one's performance is positively de-motivational. When that third party cannot be bothered to take an interest, it is even more destructive:

Barry was working in an IT division of a large company. The division had decided to "go for" ISO 9000. So Barry's unit, like others, had documented what they did and had awaited the arrival of assessors. None visited his unit. There was a sense of being let down. The division succeeded with registration, but many like Barry wondered just what it had been all about and could not share the director's pleasure at the success.

Barry, like millions of others who have been subjected to assessment, was ready to prove that he was doing what his procedures said he was doing. He was ready to show he was "doing things right", doing things according to the way they had been written down. But was he doing the right thing?

5. The Standard relies too much on people's, and in particular assessors', interpretation of quality.

The defenders of ISO 9000 acknowledge that it suffers from "problems of interpretation" in the hands of those who "know no better" — the argument always points the finger at others — and if this were the only criticism of ISO 9000 it would surely be enough to put a brake on the Standard's promulgation.

In our experience, assessors share assumptions which tell us more about their background and experience than help us understand quality. In organisations registered to ISO 9000 it is easy to find examples of "just in case" thinking, people taking an unnecessarily pessimistic view of what could go wrong; "ensure people are controlled" thinking, because you cannot trust them; "customers should all be treated the same" thinking because after all, we must be "seen to be fair". Usually these things make performance worse. They are part of a view of management which is diametrically opposed to quality, yet they have been assumed to be about quality because they have plausibility and are associated with something called a "quality standard".

Quality (following Deming) actually teaches us that you manage what could go wrong from a position of knowledge, not supposition; it teaches that people need to be in control for learning, improvement and innovation to occur; and that customers should be treated how they want to be treated — after all, the purpose of any organisation is to win and keep custom-

ers. However, this is not what is taught by ISO 9000 and its
entourage.

The sixth argument in the case against ISO 9000 is that:

6. The Standard promotes, encourages, and explicitly demands actions which cause sub-optimisation.

Dictating how customers should be treated and over-
bureaucratic documentation are two ubiquitous examples. The
requirements for control and inspection are more pernicious
forms of sub-optimisation. The consequential de-motivation —
the most debilitating form of sub-optimisation — is, in large
part, a natural response to being controlled. And ISO 9000
starts, a priori, from an attitude of control.

The need for control was the genesis of what became the
ISO 9000 movement. In the Second World War, if you wanted
to supply the Ministry of Defence with munitions, you had to
be registered to a standard upon which, ultimately, ISO 9000
was based. The intent was to prevent accidents in the munitions factories and it solved the presenting problem — bombs
were prevented from going off in factories. The approach was
to document procedures for production and ensure they were
followed through inspection. This is a way of working which
ensures that production meets specifications. It is a method of
control which ensures consistency of output. It appeared to
solve a problem of the time.

During one of many presentations of our views on ISO 9000,
we met a man who had actually worked in a munitions factory
during the War. He agreed that procedural control had solved
the presenting problem. However, he also informed us that
other features of the factories were equally hazardous, yet they
were not controlled (or prevented) because they were beyond
the scope of the requirements! It illustrates a general principle
which we use as the seventh argument in the case against ISO
9000:

7. When people are subjected to external controls, they will be inclined to pay attention only to those things which are affected by the controls.

Or, more simply: people do what you "count", not necessarily what counts. A correspondent illustrated the problem:

> *"The ISO inspectors are only shown certain areas for con-*
> *sideration — those that they know will pass. The com-*
> *pany/site then uses the ISO 9000 pass throughout as a*
> *recommendation to customers. Manuals whilst initially*
> *formatted, are not kept up to date. Records, generally, are*
> *not kept up to date. Records are often superficially modi-*
> *fied just before the next visit. I could go on. There are*
> *many small problems — no one large flaunt.*
>
> *These companies are very successful — they do not keep*
> *fully to ISO 9000, so why do we need it?"*

The main practical advantage of registration to ISO 9000 is that it enables organisations to tender for business they might otherwise not get. This is the reason managers are prepared to pay for "ready-made" manuals and obtain fraudulent assessments. It is a natural response to coercion: people "cheat" — they do what they need to do to get by, to avoid the feared consequences of (in this case) not being registered.

It is not people — workers or managers — that we should be controlling. Quality teaches us that continuous improvement relies on controlling work using different methods of control from those most managers are traditionally familiar with. At the time that our munitions factories were controlling output through ensuring that people worked to procedures, some American munitions factories were *improving* output by reducing variation. The work was led by Deming.

Following the war, Deming's ideas were ignored by American industry: a growing market tolerated the waste of inefficient production, organisations could pass their costs on to the customer. Indeed, Deming used to joke, "Let's make toast the

American way — I'll burn — you scrape!" Approaching quality
through inspection results in scraping toast. Managing
through understanding variation is the foundation for learning
and improvement. Our eighth argument in the case against
ISO 9000 is:

8. ISO 9000 has discouraged managers from learning about the theory of variation.

We have never yet met an ISO 9000 registered company which
showed an understanding and use of variation in improving
performance. Instead, ISO 9000 has encouraged managers to
believe that adherence to procedures will reduce variation.
However, as we shall demonstrate, adherence to procedures
can increase variation — registration to ISO 9000 results in
even more burnt toast! This is not to say that people should
not "do things right". Clearly there will be advantages in some
situations to working to standard procedures. But a different
view would lead one to question whether we are "doing the
right thing" and this is best determined by looking at an organisation as a system and learning from variation. We know,
for example, that product manufacturing quality improves
when variation is reduced. In service organisations, any variation from what matters to customers will similarly drive up
costs and drive away customers. Learning from variation requires measures, and measures, if chosen well and used in the
right way, lead to learning and improvement.

Managers are easily persuaded of the benefits of having
everybody working to procedures. It appears logical and com-
monsensical to think that people will do better if they are clear
about what they have to do and work is orderly. But when is
this true and when is it not true? ISO 9000 does not help us
understand the answer because it assumes that it is always
true. It starts from the presumption that it is of value to work
to procedures; procedures which are documented, showing how
work is done and inspected. ISO 9000 also provides the rules

for inspection by others to make sure that "people are doing as they should".

Deming eschewed inspection as a means to quality. The Japanese were the first to understand him. They set out to manage their organisations as systems, use measures to establish capability and improve performance through learning from variation. They out-achieved his expectations in five years. In contrast, we have had ISO 9000 / BS 5750 since 1979 — if only it had out-achieved our expectations! It is no surprise that ISO 9000 cannot compare with the success of Deming's methods in Japan, for the two are based on entirely different philosophies.

As we have just noted, the original Standard on which ISO 9000 was based was introduced in response to a crisis when bombs were exploding in factories. The wider adoption of ISO 9000 was an expedient response to a lesser crisis. Many large industrial organisations placed contractual requirements on suppliers which included requirements of their management systems. It led to suppliers being inundated with a variety of demands ostensibly to achieve the same purpose. The solution was to agree on one standard and thus the standard originally used to control munitions factories was adopted.

This is not an approach which fosters mutuality, trust and learning — the foundation for good customer–supplier relations. And this is our ninth argument in the case against ISO 9000:

9.   ISO 9000 has failed to foster good customer–supplier relations.

The Japanese learned to see their organisations as systems, systems which included suppliers and customers. From that point of view, entirely different (co-operative) thinking about how organisations, suppliers and customers can work together has developed. ISO 9000, by contrast, encourages a "contractual" view of customer–supplier relations. Suppliers are obliged to show that they are registered. People in the customer organisations become focused on doing their job as de-signed by the Standard — "I am responsible for supplier as-sessment" — obliging suppliers to register or, as we shall see, doing other things which sub-optimise customer–supplier re-lations.

ISO 9000 reinforces an "arm's length" view of management which in turn has maintained top management's ignorance about what ISO 9000 registration is doing to their operations in day-to-day practical terms. Without such first-hand knowl-edge, managers are unlikely to question either ISO 9000's or their own assumptions about how to manage. And this is the final argument in the case against ISO 9000:

10. As an intervention, ISO 9000 has not encouraged managers to think differently.

ISO 9000 has taught managers little or nothing about the most important subject on any management curriculum — quality — and it has probably made many of them averse. Some man-agers and certainly the majority of assessors believe an or-ganisation has "done quality" having registered to ISO 9000, when nothing could be further from the truth. Registration to ISO 9000 has prevented managers from learning about quality because it is no more than an expression of management thinking prevalent at the time when we began to use stan-dards to control suppliers.

ISO 9000 represents further reinforcement of the idea that work is divided into management and worker roles. We believe it was *the* fundamental mistake of twentieth-century man-agement, for ISO 9000 continues the tradition that "managers decide" and "workers do". This tradition has led to means of control — through adherence to procedures, budgets, targets and standards — which themselves cause sub-optimisation. It is a way of thinking about management which began in mass-production systems and, throughout most of this century, has been the starting point for defining the role of management.

We call this thinking "command and control". To appreciate the full extent of what ISO 9000 has done to organisations, we shall explore (in chapters 4 and 6) the nature of "command and control" management thinking and question its relevance for the problems and opportunities our organisations face today. Changing our thinking about management is the key to performance improvement. ISO 9000 does no more than encourage managers to follow a recipe which, because of its antecedents, reinforces the "wrong" thinking.

The better way starts with understanding the organisation as a system. It implies a completely different management philosophy. The Japanese companies which adopted this philosophy have achieved remarkable results. When we woke up to the "Japanese phenomenon" (in the 1970s) and sent managers to look at what they were doing, the managers copied the things they saw, such as quality circles and suggestion schemes. They could not "see" and did not understand the thinking behind what was happening. As a result, the things they copied failed — they were incompatible with the surrounding system. You cannot "do quality" in a "command and control" system.

Chapter 2

A MATTER OF OPINION

By the early 1990s over 25,000 UK organisations had been assessed and registered to ISO 9000. The Director General of the British Standards Institute asserted that these firms had improved the management of their organisations and enhanced their reputations for quality:

> *"The benefits of applying BS 5750 are real; it will save you money — because your procedures will be more soundly based and more efficient; it will ensure satisfied customers — because you have built in quality at every stage; it will reduce waste and time-consuming reworking of designs and procedures."*[*]

However, we could find no evidence to support his claims. The growth of registrations to ISO 9000 had been paralleled by a growth in debate. Management magazines, national newspapers and quality conferences had all been involved in heated discussion between the advocates and critics. It seemed to us that such discussions were generating more heat than light. Our clients' questions led us to look for research which might illuminate what was going on and help them make informed decisions about whether ISO 9000 registration would be of value. As we could find no research which could help us understand what was happening, we conducted our own.

---

[*] *BS5750/ISO9000/EN29000: 1987, A Positive Contribution to Better Business.* Executive guide to the use of national, internation and European quality standards. DTI publication.

In 1993 we published an extensive opinion survey, conducted in 647 ISO 9000 registered organisations. We now know the research suffered from problems of reliability and validity, as will become evident; but it was, nevertheless, useful in pointing us towards more fruitful lines of inquiry. The results raised interesting questions — people's perceptions may have been unreliable but the fact that these perceptions were held as opinions leads one to question why.

The 1993 research showed that only 15 per cent of the organisations surveyed believed they achieved all of the benefits claimed by the Director General of BSI; that is, improved efficiency, better procedures, less waste, lower costs and more satisfied customers. Some 69 per cent of the respondents believed that ISO 9000 improved "procedural efficiency", but the results for improvements in measurable aspects of efficiency (costs, waste etc.) were only half as good, suggesting that the improvements attributed to new procedures were coloured by opinion rather than supported by evidence. One would expect people to believe that ISO 9000 had improved their procedures — implementation of procedures is, after all, the primary focus of registration.

These were not results which encouraged confidence about ISO 9000 registration, especially when one considers that the data were being gathered from those who were likely to be well-disposed to it, the people who had championed ISO 9000 in their own organisations. The results raised questions as to whether the problems lay with the Standard, the implementers (consultants and managers) or both.

Other results from the survey can be summarised as follows:

- Most respondents (85 per cent) thought that, on the whole, ISO 9000 was a good thing, but that it suffered from problems of flexibility and interpretation.

- Governmental "customers" were more inclined to insist on supplier registration to the Standard than private sector organisations.

- Standards were set from an "internal" perspective rather than being driven by customer requirements.

- People reported that a change in culture is required to achieve success with ISO 9000 but there was a diversity of views as to whether the Standard encouraged the practice of listening to customers and whether it was important to introduce the concept of continuous improvement prior to implementation.

- People felt that the Standard had spawned many rogue consultants. Many also felt that British management did not really understand it.

- People who believed they succeeded with the Standard reported that they undertook it for broader purposes than those who undertook it mainly for reasons of obligation and opportunism.

- Smaller organisations had more concerns about costs and had greater expectations of improved market-share as a result of registration. They also had more doubts about the Standard's relevance to their business.

It seemed that although the Standard was felt to be a "good thing", there were many problems. Following the publication of this research, we visited five of the companies in the small group which had claimed ISO 9000 registration to be positive in all respects. In every case we found activity which was causing sub-optimisation, and which was present specifically because of registration to the Standard. It was a shock. It taught us not to rely on opinion data and it reminded us that managers are often out of touch with what actually happens in their organisations.

We conducted a short study among the hierarchies of these five organisations: senior management were vague but positive about the Standard, middle management had issues with practicalities and workers saw it as another management initiative which caused more (and unnecessary) work. We still did not know enough about cause and effect — what were the likely consequences if an organisation went about registration to ISO 9000? By now, fourteen years had passed since the Standard first appeared and we had no knowledge of its impact on organisation performance and competitive position. Consequently, we were unable to give our clients any more advice than we gave when they first enquired. However, we maintained our view that it was probably best avoided.

There had to be more to learn. Quality, we had come to understand, was a better way of doing business. Deming showed that as quality improved, productivity improved; it was a method of working which led organisations to greater economic security. But was ISO 9000 doing the same? Was ISO 9000 something which would benefit an organisation if approached in the right way? And if that was the case, why might some organisations succeed and others fail? Why didn't British management appear to understand it and was this important to the impact of ISO 9000 on performance? If management had understood it would they have been supportive or antagonistic?

Subsequent research conducted by Manchester Business School* and Surrey University** , both on behalf of assessing organisations, found similar results, although naturally these results were reported with a more positive "spin". The Manchester research, for example, was introduced by the sponsoring organisation with the claim that the answer to the research question was "a qualified 'yes'". Yet no data were presented which could show why or how ISO 9000 works and plenty of data were reported which might lead one to have doubts.

The Manchester research included two findings which were heralded as proof at last that ISO 9000 was beneficial. The first was that *companies with ISO 9000 certification showed a*

* "ISO9000 — does it work? A report by Manchester Business School 1995"; commissioned by SGS Yarsley International.
** "Fitter Finance. The Effects of ISO9000 on Business Performance", Commissioned by LRQA Ltd.

significantly higher rate of sales growth than the national av-erage. The claim was based on a comparison of the sales growth of registered organisations with GDP, assuming GDP to be an indicator of "all organisations'" growth. Any competent researcher would note that even if this finding were translatable into something meaningful, we would still know nothing about cause and effect. Another explanation for better sales growth in registered organisations could be that only registered organisations are able to tender for contracts; or possibly that all organisations in a sector are registered and the sector is growing.

The second "finding" was even more extraordinary. It was claimed that ISO 9000 registered organisations were *four times more likely to have survived the recent recession*. The foundation for this claim was an analysis of the progress of 185 companies which were first registered to ISO 9000 in 1991. Of the 185, 130 were still registered, 53 were still in business but no longer registered and 2 were no longer in business. This data was used to argue that the failure rate of ISO 9000 registered organisations was 1.1 per cent, which compared favourably with the national average for failures (5.2 per cent). One could equally have used this data to claim that *stopping registration to ISO 9000 won't harm your business*. It might have been more valuable to explore why the 53 decided they no longer needed to be registered to ISO 9000.

Anything more than a superficial reading of all the available research leads one to have doubts about what is going on. It is easy to see levels of dissatisfaction which are higher than ought to be tolerated, doubts about cost-effectiveness and concerns about assessors, waste (bureaucracy, paperwork, over-control) and the use of ISO 9000 as a promotional tool.

Extending ISO 9000's Reach

In 1987, BS 5750 became ISO 9000. It marked the end of a period of committee work organised by the International Organisation for Standardisation and reflected a decision to promulgate the Standard throughout the international business community. The International Organisation for Standardisation (ISO), based in Geneva, is a world-wide federation of national standards bodies whose role is to promote the development of standardisation and related activities to facilitate the international exchange of goods and services. ISO 9000 was adopted to facilitate world trade. The basis for this decision is difficult to imagine, as there was a dearth of evidence available regarding the contribution made to economic performance. We will digress to note the process of the decision: for a document to become a standard it needs to go through committee drafts; then as a "Draft International Standard" it is made available to anyone who has an interest. A final draft is prepared following representations and it is put before the membership for formal voting. A 75 five per cent vote in favour is required for acceptance. Only standards which have taken this route can be called a standard . . . except one, and that is the standard which applies to running an assessing organisation. A correspondent explained it in the following way:

> *"ISO had produced a guide for running assessing organisations. Assessment against ISO 9000 was growing around the world and there was a need to ensure that the certificates were of value; in other words that the assessing organisations were "quality-controlled". The guide was not a standard, for to be so it would have required committee stages and public consultation; this was no more than a guide produced by an appointed committee. The Centre for European Normalisation — CEN — (the ISO of Europe), took the guide and turned it into a standard. Their need was to have something for each European country's assessing organisations to be assessed against. The control of CEN is dominated by the larger European contributors, Britain amongst them. And so, in short, we found ourselves with assessing organisations which don't have to register to ISO 9000 but are instead*

assessed against what is, in effect, a simpler document,
which was not subject to the usual process for developing
standards and which has less requirements and controls."

We were often asked why assessing organisations were not
registered to ISO 9000, now we knew why. But let's return to
the purpose of this Standard: like any other adopted by the international community, it is designed to facilitate world trade.
There are two main impediments to world trade: tariffs and
technical barriers. The International Organisation for Standardisation has been responsible for breaking down the technical barriers. Harmonising international product standards
facilitates the movement of goods across boundaries and, ultimately, it reduces the cost of production. Global product standards are, it is argued, essential for a world market.

However, ISO 9000 differs from other standards in that it
relates to the management of an organisation rather than the
quality of its products. BS 5750 was the first "management
standard"; it was designed to serve a specific purpose. Government and, later, major industrial organisations wanted a
contractual document with which to manage the relationship
between buyer and seller. BS 5750 provided a model which the
customer could demand of a supplier. It was designed to put
controls in place to *assure quality*.

A Defensive Reaction

So why must we have the Standard? One correspondent explained it this way:

"Same reason as we have other standards — they can
provide protection in the contractual sphere to the extent
that, when a party claims to be operating to a standard,
then they can be held to that standard if in breach (non-
conformity to system element).

It may not be much but (a) everything that helps reduce
business risk can be worth it when the damage is large

enough and (b) between businesses, reasonable exclusion clauses can still work — if the supplier is providing product to a standard and claiming registration to ISO 9000, their exclusions cannot possibly apply to these aspects of the contract. The evidence is that businesses do not go to court about breaches of contract very often — but they do settle contractual hiccups — if one party has the legal right on their side they do have a better bargaining position."

This disturbing line of argument was noted with alarm by another correspondent:

"I mentioned I had got a book from the library. . . . You may be interested in the following extracts:

> *'ISO 9000 helps you minimise the risk of producing unsafe products. It may also give you some protection in law against product liability claims . . . all purchasers have to justify their expenditure. Things can and do go wrong, and organisations need to protect themselves against risk. If anything goes wrong, shareholders may question whether the money was spent wisely. The purchaser can say, "We checked them out. They had ISO 9000" . . . In many industries, acquiring ISO 9000 gets you on to tender lists and preferred supplier lists.'*

I find the above aspects worrying. It's almost like saying you can do murder and use ISO 9000 as a defence."

As she pointed out, the Standard does not confer immunity from legal obligations but any manager reading the book may be duped by the "experts". Another correspondent similarly argued for the "contractual" benefits of ISO 9000:

"I, the customer, specify what it is that I want and you have systems which assure me of that. If I do get what I

*want — I am satisfied — I am not interested in how effi-
ciently you managed to do it — that is your problem. If I
do not get what I specified you are in automatic and un-
excludable breach of contract."*

Is this what we want from quality? There is no doubt that
managers procuring from the defence and contracting sectors
saw the necessity for defensive and contractual relations with
suppliers, but is it necessary or even effective today? Was it
ever effective?

ISO 9000 — A Way of Managing

Quality assurance, according to the Standard, is a *way of
managing* which prevents non-conformance and thus "assures
quality". As we have noted, this is what makes ISO 9000 different from other standards: *It is a management standard, not
a product standard.* It goes beyond product standardisation: it
is standardising not *what is made* but *how it is made*. To use
standards to dictate and control how organisations work is to
extend the role of standards to new territory. To take such a
step we might have firstly established that any such requirements worked — that they resulted in ways of working which
improved performance.

Despite the lack of evidence as to whether this way of managing is better than any other, those who gain financially from
the Standard are, quite naturally, keen to promote its benefits.
One of the assessing organisations ran a series of advertise-
ments throughout 1996 claiming that ISO 9000 is *universally
recognised, improves productivity, gives an organisation a
competitive edge and pays for itself.* We (with others) com-
plained to the Advertising Standards Authority (ASA) about
the claim that ISO 9000 improves productivity. Our complaint
was upheld. But this is not a matter which should or could be
arbitrated by the ASA. They can only rely on the available information and the bulk of that is no more than opinion. The
ASA's ruling accepted the advertiser's view that ISO 9000

could improve productivity in some cases. But this takes us no further forward. In which cases and how do we know? What does a manager have to do to ensure that *their* organisation's productivity *will* improve? And if we are to accept the oft-cited view that improvements in productivity may be more difficult for small firms, what does that tell us about the Standard? How can we square this view with what Deming taught about quality — that is, that quality is a better way to improve service, costs and revenue?

From its beginnings in the UK, ISO 9000 is now extending its reach throughout the world. Today there are over 52,000 registered organisations in the UK and roughly the same number of registrations in the rest of the world. As one correspondent put it:

> *"Until recently the UK had the largest explosion of ISO 9000 take-up — it is now beginning to take off almost everywhere but particularly in the US and Germany (still not very popular in Japan)."*

Why he thought it was unpopular in Japan he didn't say, but the Japanese are not immune to the international market-forces demanding registration.

This was an approach to management which was designed to assure or, by implication, control output (stopping bombs exploding in munitions factories) and it could potentially be used to give redress when contracts were not delivered according to the original specification. For reasons best known to those who were responding to the problems of their time, it was adopted as a standard for a "quality management system".

A correspondent gave us his understanding of the history:

> *"My experience on this subject goes way back. It started when as an Engineering Manager based in the US, I found that a document called Mil-Q-9858A was being quoted to me (I still think it is a better document). Return-*

ing to the UK after a spell as Head of all technical staff, I was put in charge of the Quality organisation.

This was the time when the MoD was beginning to question the old 6/49 form conditions, so they created a document called AvP92, which was based on 9858A. Mine was the first company to be assessed to it. The other services adopted it, and it emerged as 05-21 (plus the other associated documents). In turn this series evolved into 5750, and hence ISO 9000.

I later became a Director of a UK company with specific responsibility for Quality. It was one of the first to be assessed to BS 5750. I campaigned for the adoption of a single quality standard for the automotive industry instead of small / medium companies having a succession of "assessors" descending on them. This appears finally to have happened. I always thought that this ticking boxes was a waste of resources and didn't think it did much good, but on the other hand if you did it via a third party system, it didn't do a lot of harm."

That the Standard was something which was perceived to be meeting a need is beyond doubt. Whether or not "it didn't do a lot of harm", however, is debatable. The thinking of the leaders of this movement was governed by defensive and controlling assumptions. Those who were previously referred to as "redundant government inspectors" and "surplus industry quality managers" had a hold on quality in the UK. Inevitably, these same people are the main players in the debate about how best to re-write (and improve) the Standard, the existence of such a debate itself being evidence that there are problems. Organisations have been led down the path of "quality assurance". The protagonists experienced few obstacles because this was heralded as quality.

So quality assurance was introduced to solve the problem of multiple assessments of suppliers. As the problem was perceived as a contractual problem, it made sense to those who took the decision to take an approach which sought to prevent non-conformity: "Do what you say you will do and prove that you do".

> *ISO 9000 (1994) paragraph 1: "The requirements speci-*
> *fied are aimed primarily at achieving customer satisfac-*
> *tion by preventing non-conformity at all stages from de-*
> *sign through servicing."*

To put it another way, the Standard asserts that preventing non-conformance achieves customer satisfaction. But does it? Of course it matters to customers that a product works. But there is no guarantee that the Standard will ensure even that. Furthermore, customers take a total view of an organisation — how easy it is to do business with — in respect of all things of importance to each and every customer.

ISO 9000 requires managers to "*establish and maintain a documented quality system as a means of ensuring that product conforms to specified requirements*". Loosely translated this is "say what you do". Management is supposed to "*define and document its policy for quality . . . including its commitment to quality*".

What management would not declare its commitment to quality? But would they know what it means? Would they argue (as they should) that quality management is a different and better way to do business, or would they believe that ISO 9000 will take care of quality? The Standard encourages managers to think of "quality" and "business as usual" as separate and distinct. It helps managers avoid the revelation that quality means a wholly different view of management. Instead, the organisation "*shall appoint a management representative who, irrespective of other responsibilities, shall have defined author-ity and responsibility*" [for ISO 9000]. At a practical level this means only one executive who decides he or she had better learn a thing or two about quality. It is probable that the authors of ISO 9000 saw nothing wrong with "business as usual" — and saw quality (or ISO 9000) as "extra to" business as usual not "different from".

The Standard requires organisations to conduct internal quality audits to *"verify whether quality activities comply with planned arrangements"*. This is loosely translated as "do as you say" and the purpose of the audit is to see that you do. It was not until the 1994 review that the words were changed to *"quality activities **and related results**"*. It was a Standard which was rooted in the philosophy of inspection: fifteen years after its initial promulgation the promoters sought to extend the focus to results. But results or improvements achieved by what means? Inspection? By the time the Standard was adopted world-wide, quality thinking had moved on from inspection. It is now understood, at least by a few, that quality is achieved through managing the organisation as a system and using measures which enable managers to reduce variation (see chapters 4 and 6). The defenders argue that there is nothing stopping a company having ISO 9000 and implementing methods for the reduction of variation, but where are such companies? None of the companies we have studied knew anything about this thinking. The Standard does not talk about it; moreover, the Standard effectively discourages managers from learning about it by representing quality in a different way.

It is often pointed out that "compliance with the Standard does not guarantee product or service quality". This begs the question "how *should* a management system affect the quality of an organisation's product or service"? Any such standard should provide a rationale for its requirements and, we argue, there are two distinctly different rationales: one (which has to do with control) upon which the Standard is based and another which is based on quality. The Standard requires that an organisation's chosen way of managing should be documented, such that an external (third party) assessor can check up to see that all is as it is claimed to be; inspection is the means of control. This has resulted in an industry. Assessors, trainers, committees, consultants and everybody touched by ISO 9000 are consuming time and resources which are supposed to be helping improve our competitive position. Yet we have no evidence which might assure us that we are doing the right thing and plenty of evidence suggesting otherwise.

The ISO 9000 "way of managing" is based upon the traditional, functional activities of manufacturing organisations — the Standard includes requirements for design, manufacturing, inspection, testing, delivery, installation, servicing — and the clauses are given a fairly logical progression. They are "rules" for manufacturing a product or delivering a service. These rules step beyond product quality; they move into the territory of telling managers how something should be done, something British management usually resists.

British management has been characterised by Geert Hofstede* as having a "village market mentality" preferring serendipity and opportunity as the guiding traditions, choosing order only when it has clear benefits. Hence British management's rejection of the European directives on worker participation during the early 1980s and, more recently, their antipathy towards what they see as the strictures of the Social Chapter. It is perhaps surprising that British management has not been as vociferous in their condemnation of ISO 9000. The evidence suggests this may be because they are unaware of what it is and, in any event, one cannot be seen to be "against quality". But what is quality? According to ISO 8402 (quality vocabulary), quality is:

"The totality of features and characteristics of a product or service that bear on its ability to satisfy stated or implied needs."

Everything we have learned about ISO 9000 suggests that the people who created this definition were thinking about the

---

* *Culture's Consequences: International Differences in Work-Related Values,* Sage, 1980.

things which need to be controlled, those things which "bear on its ability . . .". The builders of the Standard assumed that customer needs would be listed in contractual agreements between the supplier and customer. They accepted that in other circumstances they would be implied. In which case, they argued, the requirements must be identified and defined in order to draw up a specific quality standard. As we have seen, ISO 9000 has a "make" logic — procedures for "how you do what you do" — and a "control" logic — check to see that it is done. It is a relic of the era when contractual agreements were an important device for regulating the behaviour of suppliers. In these ways, ISO 9000 encouraged "planning for quality".

Planning for quality sounds plausible, but it assumes many things: that the plan is the right plan, that it is feasible, that people will "do it", that performance will improve. It is an approach which, paradoxically, leads to poor decisions. Planners of quality systems, guided by ISO 9000, start with a view of how the world should be as framed by the Standard. Understanding how an organisation is working, rather than how someone thinks it should is a far better place from which to start change of any kind (as we will show in chapter 7).

Improvement, Tinkering or Maintaining the Status Quo?

Even the promulgators and defenders of ISO 9000 are open about what they see to be the Standard's limitations. They would not go so far as to stop it, perhaps not least because many of them are dependent on the Standard for their living. They argue that, with improvements, the Standard will serve its purpose. It interests us to note that the implicit failure which this line of argument accepts is never quantified, measured or costed. It is one thing to declare that ISO 9000 needs improving, but how will we know it has improved if we have no measure of the extent of its current failure? Should we simply have faith?

The 1994 revision included (for the first time) the requirement for *continuous improvement,* not saying much about "by what method" (a central issue for Deming) and begging the question why it hadn't been included before. The next revisions are expected to be published in the year 2000. The body responsible for revisions (ISO technical committee 176) claims to be listening to the "voice of the customer". In *Quality Online* (January 1997) [http://www.qualitymag.com], TC 176 is reported to have learned from its customers that ISO 9000 needs to *"improve confidence in outcomes and value relative to the implementation effort"*. In plain language this can only mean customers are worried about whether it works and whether it is worth the effort. Their customers were also reported as saying that the review needs to *"improve applicability to a broad range of organisational sizes and range of products"* and needs to *"improve flexibility of use and user-friendliness"*. These needs indicate customers are having problems with use.

TC 176 has created new vision and mission statements:

"Our vision is that, through its world-wide acceptance and use, the ISO 9000 family of standards will provide an effective means for improving the performance of individual organisations and providing confidence to people and organisations that products (goods and services) will meet their expectations thereby enhancing trade, global prosperity, and individual well-being."

The mission is to:

"Identify and understand user needs in the field of quality management, develop standards that respond effectively to the expectations of users, support implementation of these standards, and facilitate meaningful evaluation of the resulting implementations."

The reader may have noticed the explicit assumption that ISO 9000 is here to stay. If TC 176 were really listening to their customers would there not be a stronger emphasis on "meaningful evaluation of implementation"? Just suppose for a moment that ISO 9000 was a product. Would it be reflective of a quality attitude to keep obliging people to buy a product when the users complain of cost effectiveness and usability? Perhaps if the marketplace obligation were ceased, this "product" would die a natural death. There seems to be little intrinsic value to the customer.

Each time the Standard has been revised, the critics have maintained that it continues to show the same weaknesses — that it is too "unfriendly" to use, has too many documents and is administered by assessors who show poor understanding, which leads in turn to poor quality assessments. You would have thought these criticisms alone would be enough to call a halt to the promulgation of the Standard as a necessary requirement for doing business. The consistent criticism of "poor quality auditing" resulted in the birth of "Tickit", a standard which applies to software development organisations. It was an attempt to deal with the problem of assessors: where they came from, the advice they brought and their impact on registering organisations. This is how it was put to us:

"There had been a lot of questions and concerns about assessors. It was obvious that we needed better ones, but to try to control what had become a burgeoning population would be difficult, if not impossible. The answer was to try to improve the quality of assessing in just one sector and the IT sector was chosen because everybody expressed concerns about the performance of software products and the potential gains from quality improvement in software products were significant. The revisionists argued that assessors should not be full-time appointments (to get away from the 'surplus Government inspectors') but instead should be employed on a part-time basis, using people with jobs in the particular industry. At this time there were other problems that needed to be solved. BSI (British Standards Institution) had the lion's share of the assessment market in the UK and had the advantage of being

associated with the 'kite mark', something people were familiar with as it had been applied to products for generations; it was not easy for new entrants to get established in the assessment business. Creating another 'mark' could solve the problem. Tickit represented a 'better' accreditation scheme, designed to exert better control of the assessing organisations. Auditors had to meet strict criteria, had to complete a specific course relating to ISO 9000 assessment in the IT sector and were selected by a panel. The Tickit scheme published a customer guide (what you can expect from ISO 9000), a supplier guide (how to conduct ISO 9000 for your software organisation), and an auditor's guide (designed to encourage consistency of auditing).

In addition, the Tickit scheme included three-yearly complete audits, a change from the usual practice where, once registered, an organisation only experiences part-audits. Needing to undertake a full review every three years, it was felt, would precipitate greater competition in the market as organisations would be more likely to shop around. In truth, and if it works, all Tickit represents is a better application of ISO 9000."

An unanticipated consequence of Tickit has been discontent at the rule that organisations producing software must be assessed through the Tickit scheme. As more and more products include software, the non-Tickit assessing organisations are getting uncomfortable. They are seeing themselves being squeezed out of their markets.

But has Tickit solved the problem? We have no hard evidence either way. We have nothing to guide us except the opinions of those who have control of the ISO 9000 movement. Shouldn't TC 176 be working on why there are problems of these kinds? Isn't this where *"meaningful evaluation of implementation"* would be of value? The most recent meeting of TC 176 (November 1996 for a week in Tel Aviv) was spent discussing convergence: convergence of ISO 9002 and ISO 9003 with ISO 9001; convergence of QS 9000 with ISO 9000; convergence of ISO 9000 with ISO 14000 (an environmental standard). TC 176 claims to be listening to its customers but spends its time on other issues — or are we to believe that convergence will solve the problems of cost-effectiveness and usability?

TC 176 spends time on convergence because it is the stuff of the standards movement; it is the flavour of the moment. As new standards are being developed for health and safety and environmental issues, the revisionists want to incorporate them all into general standards for doing business. Where is the evidence that shows us this is a sensible thing to do? We fear that convergence will only result in building a larger army of more broadly based assessors. There is little evidence of the likely impact on the matters they would be sent out to address.

A further criticism, to which the "convergence" argument is responding, is that the Standard does not include "business management"; that is, the requirements are regarded as separate from the day-to-day operations of running a business — how a business makes its money. The antecedents show us that the original thinking behind the Standard was focused exclusively on the means of production, it was a focus on manufacturing procedures. As we have noted, the separation of quality from business is a reinforcement of the view that quality is something "extra" rather than a different or better way of running a business. Another way to put it is that financial control is separate from process control. This is to separate costs from the causes of costs — to concentrate on the former is representative of a logic built from "command and control" thinking, the major impediment to quality in organisations.

Those who appreciate this problem usually argue that the Standard requires additional clauses to prescribe business management processes. It is a worrying response: we have yet to establish the validity of the current clauses; to issue further "business prescriptions" could exacerbate an already difficult situation. Moreover, new prescriptions could continue to separate "business" and "process". Once again, such a separation is reflective of "command and control" management thinking.

Another "convergence" argument is that the usability of the Standards will improve with their simplification. The starting place for this argument is a recognition that the current standards still reflect their origins in large-scale engineering organisations with conventional hierarchical structures. Organisational structure was and still is a potential impediment to quality management. The idea is that it should have generic applicability and should be written in a way which is manifestly applicable to and recognisable by the widest possible range of organisations. To have value across a wide range of circumstances, it is argued, the Standards should avoid stipulating requirements that are specific to particular organisations or industries. This argument goes on to assert that a generically applicable standard could be used by all organisations provided they first set about selecting and defining those elements which were of importance for their particular circumstances. The advantage is that they would avoid the problem of having to be compliant with requirements which are irrelevant in their case and would avoid the excesses of "picky" assessors. To be successful, such a standard would have to have identified the "essentials" for a quality system and make no distinction between this and the business management system. It is a worthwhile approach but it suffers the weakness of needing agreements of interpretation between the organisation and its assessors, which itself has been a cause of many problems.

In the year 2000, the revision of ISO 9000 will be published. Who will have the final say? It is inevitable that those who have control will argue that their revisions take due account of the matters raised. But are they responding to what matters to their customers or doing what they exist to do, regardless of consequences? We believe TC 176 should be encouraging communication about the nature of failure and, if they can find them, publicising examples of success showing how, in practical terms, ISO 9000 should be done. They should be acknowledging the problems of cost-effectiveness and addressing the practical concerns experienced by managers. If TC 176 were to give strong leadership on these issues they would be less open to the charge of exercising a vested interest behind closed doors. People notice when a group holds sway over popular opinion: they start to question who these people are and by what authority they act. Many correspondents have commented on the extent of institutional and economic interests in ISO 9000.

By the year 2000 we will have been employing (nay, foisting) a Standard in (on) our organisations for 22 years, with what total effect no-one really knows. The only thing we know for sure is that each revision has meant additional costs for participating organisations — minimally in terms of purchasing the revisions and much more so in updating documentation to comply with new requirements. The people working on the revisions accept that there are problems and some seek our participation in the review. One put it this way:

> *"The debate on the design spec. for ISO 9000 has started. If you are so anti, as you claim, why not let us have what you believe should be the specification for quality. You keep challenging us to defend the Standard as it is. I challenge you to tell us what is wrong, why and what should be done to put it right. The challenge also includes the requirement that you must not refer to anything to do with certification but only to ISO 9000 and its associated documents on the understanding that if you follow them you should establish a good management system."*

We could not say what should be done to put it right. There are three reasons. The first is that we think it is fallacious to assume that we can "get it all right" in a document. If that were possible it would have been done by now. Secondly, assuming that we could write a perfect prescription, the written word is probably the weakest method of intervention for changing someone's view of the world — we should not expect that people will follow a prescription. Thirdly, the above respondent separates "certification" (registration) from the Standard. At one level this is a recognition that many of the "certifiers" (assessors) have been responsible for leading organisations to do things which they would have better avoided — there are those who would have us believe that it is only the assessors who are bringing the Standard into disrepute. To have accepted this invitation would have been to ignore the importance of practical evidence. We believe we can only learn if we keep theory and practice together.

We Still Know Very Little

And so the debate goes on. The implementation of ISO 9000 is leading to confusion rather than learning. The leaders of the ISO 9000 movement are seeking to separate "registration" from "the Standard", as though this will protect their legitimacy. They do not appear to be as astonished as us that criticisms of understandability and usability should be current after all this time. If Deming could communicate a way of looking at and improving work to a group of Japanese industrialists who translated his theory into action and got results in four years, it begs the question: Are we communicating badly or communicating the wrong thing? Deming did not communicate a prescription but a way of thinking. The consequences were learning and improvement.

To learn more about what was happening with ISO 9000 we knew we had to change our approach. Rather than rely on opinion data, we took to studying individual organisations to learn from what they had done. We were interested in why they had done it, how they had done it and what the consequences were for their organisation. But before we look at the case studies, we shall explore what the defenders of the Standard say.

Chapter 3

IN DEFENCE OF THE STANDARD

Advertising has been telling managers that ISO 9000 registration is not only a "good thing", but also a necessity. Governmental and larger organisations have been obliging their suppliers to register and yet the overwhelming evidence would suggest we should be more cautious. When we published our 1993 research we joined the debate and, it has to be said, we took the view that ISO 9000 registration was a mistake. We argued that if, as a business community, we were committed to quality, then surely we would want to be satisfied that anything we were doing to improve it was tried and tested or "fit for purpose". To carry on with something which was clearly showing equivocal results would not be a "quality" response, but rather was tantamount to burying one's head in the sand while industry was suffering.

The opinion and anecdotal data, together with what we found in every case we studied, were suggesting that registration to ISO 9000 was a guarantee of sub-optimising performance. It seemed to us that this "emperor" had no clothes. We took this view to those who were promoting the Standard as an essential tool for quality improvement. When you publicly criticise something which has been taken for granted, you expect to be under attack from those who have a vested interest. We were. It is regarded by many as audacious and irresponsible to criticise ISO 9000. In a nutshell, we have argued that this Standard has nothing to do with quality and that it is damaging economic performance and, thus, our competitiveness. This has not gone down well with the Standard's defenders.

When confronted with the evidence of failure, the defenders argue that ISO 9000 is no more than a first step on the quality journey, but should this mean that we should not expect improvement? Do we have to go backwards before we go forwards? Should we tolerate a worsening of performance? And if so, for how long? Some argue "you have to do it right", others argue that ISO 9000 needs to be accompanied by a culture change — a seemingly illusive influence which prevents organisations from changing and a label which, in our experience, leads managers to accept any plausible offering which claims to change a culture.

Many arguments in defence of ISO 9000 are no more than rationalisations of the failure of registration to make a difference. ISO 9000 consultants lead the "you have to do it right" school. Internal quality advisors and human resources personnel are amongst those who argue that "change takes time", or they assert that "ISO 9000 is no more than an element in their total change programme", as though this legitimises worsening performance and other obvious problems. We argue that such rationalisations prevent learning.

Why does performance not change as was intended? Is the intention of the Standard to lead to better performance? Why will it? How much time should this change take? How do the elements of ISO 9000 impact performance and why? If we don't ask and answer these questions we will be unlikely to learn. If we do not learn we are more likely to continue to waste resources and undermine our competitive position. The cost of failure goes far beyond the price tag of registration. Unhappy customers and the demoralisation of staff are frequent and costly consequences of failure.

It is significant that not one manager has told us we've got it wrong, although to be fair a few have wondered at our absolute conviction that ISO 9000 damages performance, having themselves seen order emerge from chaos or other similar "minimal" outcomes. Most managers who have joined the debate have either expressed similar misgivings to ours or have shown that they are interested in obviating what they see to be the Standard's disadvantages. Most of the managers we meet are concerned to improve performance and they see ISO 9000 as an impediment. The advantages pointed to by the few boil down to "improving clarity" (of procedures), or being able to tender for work. Few managers claim that ISO 9000 improves business performance and many of the people who do — who tend not to be managers — are too remote from where the work is done to know.

The defenders put forward a number of arguments. None is satisfactory and together these arguments only add to our conviction that we have a serious problem on our hands. If the performance of UK plc was not at stake it would not matter very much. But it is and it does. So what is said in defence of ISO 9000?

"It's OK if you do it properly."

This is at least an implicit recognition of the fact that people are having problems. Is it a satisfactory defence? The argument goes that "proper implementation is vital" and "interpretation is not the fault of the Standard". It probably goes without saying that this is the favourite argument of those who make their living from ISO 9000. They would have us believe that there are good and bad ways of "doing ISO".

It is a terrible argument. How many good ways? How many bad? How will we know? Who can we trust to tell us? How many have suffered at the hands of bad advice or misguided interpretation and what has this already done to competitive performance? How is a manager to make a choice? How can it be a decision based on the confidence that one can predict an improvement in performance? Should managers just soldier on in the hope that they hit on the right answers or find the right advice? How many sources of advice should they tap before they are satisfied that the one they choose to follow is the right thing to do for their business?

"It's OK if you do it properly" is not a sustainable defence. Furthermore, it ignores the evidence that shows how the Standard specifically encourages actions which cause sub-optimisation of performance.

"ISO 9000 is a minimum standard or a 'first step' on the quality journey."

Taking the notion of the Standard being a minimum, one correspondent said:

> *"I stress minimum because failure to recognise this important aspect leads to misplaced anger when results do not stack up to expectations."*

It interested us that this correspondent implied that managers should be warned that they should not expect too much from ISO 9000. We would want managers to expect a lot from quality. After all, it is a far better way to run a business. But is the Standard a "first step"? The notion that ISO 9000 is a minimum standard implies that there is a continuum — it is often expressed thus: "quality starts with ISO 9000, and progresses through TQM to World Class".

For there to be a continuum, one should be satisfied that points on the continuum reflect ever greater degrees of the underlying principle or philosophy. That is, "World Class" operations should show the same basic principles as ISO 9000 registered operations only in greater degree. However, in every case we have studied, ISO 9000 registration has, for example, maintained the division of labour between doing work and decision-making. Every case has also maintained measures which are associated with a traditional "command and control" view of the organisation. In World Class operations, decision-making is in the hands of people who do the work and they use different measures from those we are used to in "command and control" organisations, and these alternative measures are essential prerequisites for flexibility and learning. To understand how to make such changes, managers need to change their thinking about measurement. To do that, they have to change their thinking about how to run an organisation. Changing from "command and control" to "World Class" means a change in management thinking. Ironically, adopting the Standard in no way triggers that change; indeed, it hinders it.

The distinction is philosophical. It is about the management, or more specifically the control, of organisations. The thinking about control implicit in ISO 9000 is diametrically opposed to the thinking about control in World Class operations. What we have learned is that putting control of processes in the hands of people doing the work results in more learning, pride and, in fact, more and better control.

ISO 9000 is predicated on the plausible idea that procedures are the prerequisite for control. One correspondent expressed it this way:

"We all work to procedures in some way, form or other in our daily lives. Voluntarily and involuntarily. Our own individual life style in the modern world is built around procedures. Some written in law and others by habit or etiquette. Without the visible and invisible rules we would surely drop into chaos.

This analogy can be equally applied to the work place in any environment. The company takes the view that it wishes to make money. In order to do that it must make or do something that attracts customers. To maintain customers and to broaden its sales area it must go on satisfying customers. To ensure that this philosophy is understood by all a policy is established which is supported by a set of rules that govern output. The management maintain control over its production or service. Discipline is maintained and output stabilised."

This is the "bomb factory" argument. Control of procedures will control output. But quality is concerned with improving output. Another correspondent understood this distinction:

> *"In its basic form it is a tool that can be used as the foundation of a control structure that regulates and introduces consistent operations within an organisation. An approved system can go a long way to giving assurance to a customer that there is some level of control on how operations are conducted. It does not, and never has, assured good quality output."*

Should we be heartened that the output of our organisations is controlled or dismayed that we have stifled learning, innovation, flexibility, improvement and damaged our competitive position? When we embarked on this journey did we seek "control" or "improvement"? Perhaps this is at the heart of the problem: a standard which solved a control problem was subsequently labelled as a solution to quality problems. There is a discontinuity between the theory of control as expressed in ISO 9000 and the theory of control as expressed in World Class operations.

There is a further argument used by those with a "procedural-control" view of the world:

> *"Before a process can be improved, it must be established as a set of procedures which people conform to."*

This may have value for a new process but for existing operations we differ strongly. The first thing that should be done if one seeks improvement is to find out what is currently going on and why. This can only be done through measurement — measures of what the process (or processes) is predictably achieving, perhaps also measures of what is predictably going wrong. Only if a process is entirely unpredictable might it be necessary to establish and work to procedures in order to learn more about what is going on. When you set about establishing the capability of processes (what they are predictably achieving) in "command and control" organisations, you often find that they are stable but exhibit wide variation. The variation is, most often, caused by "tampering" — managers paying attention to output data (targets, standards, budgets) causing people to "do whatever it takes" to meet the required numbers. Measures of work are often distorted by managers who bring work backwards or forwards in order to "make their numbers". Variation caused by such tampering only makes it harder to learn about what is going on in the process(es) (we return to the theory of variation in chapter 4).

The argument for first establishing procedures reflects a control view of the world. By contrast, to establish what is happening, and why, is to start from a position of wanting to learn. To establish what is happening and why requires managers to take different measures and use them differently, it requires that they understand the theory of a system and how to learn from variation (see chapters 4 and 6).

Management behaviour is governed by management thinking. Which is why the next argument used by the defenders is so disturbing:

"ISO 9000 is no more than a management tool."

The problem is it is a tool crafted by people who think of management in a particular way. To argue that ISO 9000 is no more than a management tool is to assume that it is an appropriate tool and, if it is, that the managers know how to use it to best effect. This argument takes no account of the nature of the tool.

One defender who subscribed to this view described ISO 9000 in the following way:

> *"1. It sets a basic level of customer assurance through certification.*
>
> *2. It enables management to visibly apply the invisible rules they always had.*

3. The exercise buys the workforce into the scheme; thus it becomes self-perpetuating.

Lest we forget our focus."

Taking each of his arguments in turn: There is plenty of evidence to show that certification (we are using the term "registration") cannot be relied upon to assure much. It might be what was intended, but registration is no more than a form of control and, as such, can be relied upon to guarantee little or nothing. People are adept at getting around controls. A host of organisational behaviour from "buying ISO 9000 as a ready-made manual" to the unholy rush to be in order for the assessor is caused by the fact of obligation to keep registration. Even those organisations which do not "cheat" will, because of ISO 9000, establish controls in their businesses which may or may not be creating value for their customers and hence may prevent rather than facilitate performance improvement.

To assert that ISO 9000 enables management to "visibly apply the rules they always had" is precisely our point. ISO 9000 is no more than a particularly inefficient application of traditional management thinking — it sets out to control people's behaviour through procedures and inspection — the very thinking which needs to change if we are to establish quality as a way of life in our organisations.

To take his third point: although we hear a lot about "workforce participation" in ISO 9000 registration we have yet to meet a workforce which speaks well of working to the requirements of the Standard. On the contrary, ISO 9000 has been a major cause of demoralisation and it is easy to see why. In most cases the work procedures have been imposed on the workforce. It is argued that the enlightened way to go about registration is to have the workers involved in writing their own procedures. But in these cases too the consequence is often a lowering of morale. ISO 9000 imparts a philosophy of working to procedures rather than working to improve performance.

Finally, to argue as he does that ISO 9000 is of value in reminding people of the organisation's focus is to place value on the "contract" between them and their customer and the associated "procedures" for its delivery. This is not a quality focus, it is no more than focusing on "doing what we say we do". The value created by organisations for their customers goes beyond the performance against contract. The customers' view of any organisation is made up of the whole range of transactions they experience. The focus of an organisation wanting to improve quality and competitive position should be on learning not compliance.

The idea that organisations should adhere to their contracts with customers is laudable and would be a significant benefit to our competitive position whether it were achieved through ISO 9000 registration or any other means. But ask any manager about their experiences of ISO 9000 registered companies and you will find plenty of evidence which casts doubts on the claim that ISO 9000 is a guarantee of an organisation's ability to meet its contractual obligations.

ISO 9000 is not a minimal Standard, it is a minimalist Standard. It may have had value as a basic control of suppliers at a time when there were no better methods, but today it reinforces the message that it is management's job to decide and the workers' job to do. As a management tool it is no more or less than "more of the same" — it is "command and control" by prescription.

"There is no choice, it is a requirement for doing business."

A real but sad reflection of what has occurred in the British marketplace. The same is now happening across the world; an American correspondent put it this way:

> *"It's like a freight train coming down the tracks — you're either on it or on the tracks."*

People now believe it is an absolute requirement (despite evidence to the contrary). The growth in registrations has been achieved through market-place coercion, by instilling fear of what may happen if an organisation does not register. The only way to diminish coercion is to create a wave of opinion against it. The few that have not succumbed to coercion have not lost out. In fact they have won. They are without the encumbrance of the Standard, they have not felt the need to argue as others have done:

"It is important for defensive reasons."

This argument goes that we need ISO 9000 for the same reason as we have other (product) standards — they can provide protection in the contractual sphere to the extent that, when a party claims to be operating to a standard, then they can be held to that standard if in breach (non-conformance). We are ill-served by a contractual and defensive view of customer–supplier relationships, and even though the Standard can be used as a card in disputes between customers and suppliers, few do so because the Standard does not and cannot guarantee the quality of the product nor even that the product will be delivered on time. The real defence is avoiding being the odd one out. Everybody's doing it because everybody's doing it:

"It must be good, 100,000 companies can't be wrong."

We have over 52,000 registrations in the UK, the remainder are spread around the world. There are no data other than opinion data to show that it has any value in terms of organisation performance but it has been promulgated as worthy and so it must be good because everybody says it is good. Organisations are abiding by a requirement when there is no evidence that it is the right thing to do. In the American civil war field surgeons swore by their methods which, because of their ignorance of germs, were actually killing many of the wounded they treated. This is analogous to the situation we have with ISO 9000. It is making the patient's condition worse, but it re-

flects the views of those who control the quality movement —
the "field surgeons". How many "patients" have to die before
we take a look at what is going on?

The defenders of the Standard would have us believe that
the Standard cannot be blamed, as though this was a reason to
defend it's promulgation:

> *"It is not the Standard ipso facto but its use which has so*
> *seriously gone wrong (bearing in mind that there are well*
> *known defects in the Standard which are at present being*
> *addressed). For this I have sympathy with the right-*
> *minded but poor consultancy-duped managers, but not*
> *too much for the cynical "I'll have a bit of that" managers*
> *who don't want to know what that is or how they have to*
> *change their attitude to implement it properly."*

Leaving aside the problems of "it's OK if you do it right" implicit in his first argument, he is right. He asserts that it has
gone seriously wrong. Whether the defects are "well known"
(especially by managers, the constituency which ought to
know) and will be addressed, is left open to question. He is
right to say that managers' attitudes need to change if they are
to understand quality. But managers have to be helped with
an explanation of how their attitudes need to change and
many who have experienced the excesses of the Standard will
already have negative attitudes to what has been sold to them
as "quality".

The same correspondent laid the blame at the drivers behind the ISO 9000 movement:

> *"I would suggest that much of the problem can be once*
> *again laid before our wonderful ministers primarily at*
> *the DTI but the rest of the gang are equally implicated in*
> *pushing something that they did not understand at all.*
> *They did not know (a) how complex a "proper" implemen-*
> *tation is, but (b) they seem to somehow have done the*

> *double trick of taking on the fact without knowing it be-*
> *cause they operated an almost total NIMBY attitude, solv-*
> *ing civil service troubles by privatisation instead of TQM*
> *implementation."*

His first point is a familiar one; there are those who claim they
"know" what proper implementation means; it is the belief
which lies behind "its OK if you do it right". His second point
raises an interesting argument. Would the long-term consequences be better if we had kept (for example) our utilities as a
single system and improved it rather than breaking them up
into a series of smaller systems and encouraging them to compete? The long-term consequences of privatisation are yet to
arrive. Government can produce statistics which show the
short-term gains from privatisation (and these are open to
question), but in the long term privatisation and competitive
tendering could mean greater cost. Ex-public service organisations now have greater and often duplicate infrastructures. To
have improved their performance with a minimal or single in-
frastructure might have been a far better strategy for the long-
term economic good.

But it does not help to lay the blame on government. If we
did, government would be obliged to turn to the decision-
makers of the quality movement. If they did, they would find
equivocation, defensiveness and the assertions that "it will be
all right eventually" or "change takes time". But the evidence
suggests that change through ISO 9000 makes performance
worse. The defenders ignore the practical evidence. When presented with what has actually happened in practice they
blame anything or anyone rather than accept that we have a
problem. What is extraordinary is that people who work in organisations will readily acknowledge that there is a problem,
but the "ISO 9000 industry" has a critical mass which makes it
appear deaf and unstoppable. The mountain of institutions,
experts, publications and organisation appointees which con-

stitute this "industry" casts a very large shadow over the evidence of what is happening.

The momentum continues through the promised revisions which, as we said, are at least something of an acknowledgement of failure. We should not assume that to change the requirements — re-writing the Standard — will result in organisations following the better prescription. What is required in management is a change in thinking. Managers need to be persuaded that their current "view" of their organisation is the thing that needs to change. They need to discover that their current view of the world is wrong, or at best limiting, and is blinding them to a different, better, view.

In order to improve performance, organisations registered to ISO 9000 will have to unlearn and undo much of what they have implemented. They will first need to learn how to understand their organisation as a system.

Chapter 4

THE ORGANISATION AS A SYSTEM

It was in the early 1950s that Deming showed the Japanese how to understand and run their organisations as systems. He explained that we should not think of organisations as functional hierarchies with budgetary controls. He persuaded his audience to think again about something which (in Western industrialised countries) had become "normal". Deming eschewed the thinking and practices of traditional mass production organisations, showing how their methods resulted in suboptimisation. This is not to say that mass production systems did not (and do not) work; they were an innovation which resulted in great improvements in productivity. His argument was that organisations could improve further but only by taking a different view, a systems view.

Aside from those few who have followed Deming's teachings, twentieth century managers have developed a philosophy or way of thinking and behaving which we have come to call "command and control" management. "Command and control" thinking is still the modus operandi for most of our organisations today. It is not to do with being "bossy". It is a logic about how to run an organisation and it pervades the way we think about and manage work. Command and control management thinking begins with the separation of "decision-making" from "doing" and hence it defines management's role (as decision-making). Work is typically designed in functional specialisms and "control" or decision-making is exercised through financial budgets or work targets and standards. The work of manage-

ment becomes "paying attention to output": monitoring of
numbers, standards or specifications, in the false but plausible
assumption that improving the numbers is the same as improving performance. As Deming taught, it is a way of managing which guarantees sub-optimisation. It causes waste, it
prevents managers from understanding how and why their organisations perform as they do. Consequently, managers can
often act in ways which makes things worse. Worst of all, it is
a way of managing which damages morale.

We believe that "command and control" management
thinking must be abandoned. If it is not, our organisations will
remain sub-optimised and even more importantly, their
"creative anarchy" will never be unleashed; we will not learn,
innovate and change. Without optimisation, learning, innovation and change we will cease to compete effectively in the
world economy.

> *There is a story about a Japanese guru, working with the
> board of management of a British organisation. His job
> was to recommend how they could improve performance.
> He prepared a list of recommendations and the first rec-
> ommendation was "the board should resign". He got the
> board's attention, but the point he wanted to make was "if
> you don't change your thinking, nothing will change".*

People's behaviour is governed by the system they work in. In
turn, the system is governed by the prevailing management
thinking. Interestingly, this helps us understand why so many
programmes of change fail. When they fail it is generally because the attempt was non-systemic — there was no change to

the system and, by implication, no change to management thinking. Change in performance requires a change to the system and to change the system, management have to change the way they think.

Understanding why change programmes fail is one way to get to grips with systems thinking. Often they fail when people are trained and put back into a system which is not designed to "let them do it". To take a simple example: training everybody in customer care assumes that if people do "as they have been trained" with customers, customer service will improve. In practice, the behaviour of people who deal with customers is governed by their system. It is management who put in place the work functions, information, roles, procedures and measures which create the system which either helps or impedes service and learning (improvement). It is the system which is often, in fact, preventing change.

For example, should a service engineer be in your home and unable to repair your appliance, his behaviour at that point will be determined by the system he works in. There are three things in a service engineer's system: call despatch, who tell him where to go; logistics, who provide him with parts, and his manager. If each of these parts of the system is designed to fulfil its own purpose, rather than the common purpose — if call-despatch people are measured on calls they take, their focus becomes "take calls", not help the engineers to route efficiently and meet commitments to customers; if logistics is measured on inventory costs, so they make it difficult for engineers to get spares and the decision to hold spares is always made on the basis of cost, not service to the customer; if managers are measuring engineers' activity, assuming that increasing activity increases productivity — the engineer will be unable to make and meet a commitment to you, the customer. In a badly designed system, no amount of customer-service training for engineers will make a difference.

The failure of programmes of change is masked by both the plausible aspiration to "do things right" and the rationalisation that "change takes time". Unfortunately, there is not much questioning as to whether the programmes were the "right things to do". Many programmes of change, despite the fact that they appear to have the right labels ("customer care", "quality", "co-operation", "teamwork"), fall far short of success because there is no change to the system. In the case of ISO 9000, the focus of implementation is typically "what do we need to do to achieve registration?", regardless of whether these actions will facilitate or impede performance improvement. In chapter 7 we explore the practical consequences of following the usual prescription when implementing ISO 9000: for now we need to establish what it means to understand and act on an organisation as a system — and contrast this with traditional "command and control" management thinking — because it is from this "systems" perspective that we develop our case against ISO 9000.

Function or Flow?

A system is a whole made up of parts. Each part can affect the way other parts work and the way all parts work together will determine how well the system works. What matters is how work flows through the system and how the parts of the system affect that flow. Taking this view has profound implications for what it means to manage. Traditionally we have learned to manage an organisation by managing its separate (functional) pieces (sales, marketing, production, logistics, service etc.). Managing in this way always causes suboptimisation. Parts achieve their goals at the expense of the whole; people do what they have to do to "make their numbers" (for example, "sell what you can get away with"), even if this means a loss to the system (poor quality sales resulting in returns and/or customer dissatisfaction).

"Outside-in" Rather than "Top-down"

A systems view of an organisation starts from the outside-in. How does this organisation look to its customers? How easy is it to do business with? The focus is: how well does the system respond to the demands made on it by its customers? To begin an analysis of an organisation as a system, the place to start is at the points of transaction with the customer.

For example, how does an intruder alarm company look from the outside-in? To keep it simple, we will start at the point when a salesman has been given an order. We must assume that the customer is happy, he or she has parted with half of the payment (common practice in selling intruder alarms). Next the customer sees an installation engineer. We want to know what happens predictably now. How often does the engineer arrive on time as committed to the customer? How often is the engineer able to complete his task without a hiccup? Here's what we found in one particular case:

> *There were many customers complaining that they were waiting for installation. We found that when installing, the engineer had to ask customers about the siting of equipment — things the customer had covered with the salesman — and, furthermore, the engineer often found that he did not have sufficient equipment to complete the job.*

What is Predictable?

A systems view leads managers to ask: what is predictable about the process — what will predictably happen in the future if nothing changes? Management by prediction is the hallmark of systems thinking. How predictably do these problems occur? In this case we found there were no jobs which went without a hiccup at installation. One hundred percent failure, predictably. Which means that if nothing is changed the same will happen in the future, next week and the week after. Imagine the costs — the costs of bad "word-of-mouth" from custo͏ͅ ͘ers who are not happy waiting, the inefficiency associated with having to return for equipment, the impact on the customer of being asked the same thing twice. (Also note that few of these costs will be seen in traditional, functional measures.) Now we have to ask why this is happening. The fact that it is common and predictable is good news (however bad the impact) because if something is happening predictably, it is being caused by the system and that is under management's control. In this case it was easy to see why.

Salespeople were targeted on revenue. Because they were focused on "making their numbers", rather than ensuring that the organisation delivered a quality service, they would do anything to get a sale; for example, leave cabling underestimated (to keep the price down) or specify insufficient parts. They would also tend to leave documentation in an unfinished state, causing administration to search for missing information before scheduling an engineer. Branch managers were targeted on revenue. They allocated work to installation schedules according to its contribution to their budget, not commitments already made to customers. When the engineer came on site they would often have to re-do the salesperson's work; they might have to ask the customer about the siting of equipment or would have to return for more equipment.

You will recall that the customer parted with half of the payment at the time of sale. The second payment was triggered by the original installation date. Delays to the installation schedule caused by branch manager's attention to revenue meant that some customers would receive a demand for the second payment before installation. This was the biggest cause of customer complaints. Documenting the procedures of this system will not have improved anything, and it might have made things worse.

As it happens, the organisation on which this example is based was registered to ISO 9000; it had to be to satisfy the requirements of its industry regulator. The ISO 9000 defenders argue that, for example, keeping the salespeople "controlled" by administration refusing to accept uncompleted or inaccurate forms will improve things. In our experience it only leads to increased conflict between administration and sales (and did so in this case); it is no more than an attempt to control symptoms — to deal with problems caused by the system. The causes of failure we have identified so far were mostly due to the way the organisation used measures. They were used to monitor and control functions; weekly reports would show numbers for revenue and costs. It may have come to the reader's attention that they were not really achieving control in terms of what was happening for the customer. The system's failures were, quite naturally, causing more demands from its customers — customers were progress-chasing and complaining. To establish a set of procedures for handling customer complaints (a favourite demand of ISO 9000 assessors) would only miss the point — all of this dysfunctional activity was caused by the way the organisation worked. The priority has to be to change the way it works. To reveal the failures one has to look outside-in, one has to see how the parts worked together. One has to look at the organisation as a system. It is axiomatic to a systems perspective that it would be more efficient and better for future revenues to make and meet commitment to customers, to agree and deliver without causing waste.

An administration division of a life insurance company received a lot of calls from the field sales force. The sales force was unhappy about how quickly the calls were handled. The organisation had (foolishly)* introduced service standards but they were not being met. A meeting was or-

---

* To establish a service standard without first establishing capability is gambling with two possibilities: first, that the standard is beyond the current capability and will not be met, causing distortion and complaints; second, that the standard is below current capability, being easily met and thus putting an artificial ceiling on performance — see pp. 73–75.

*ganised between the managers from sales and admini-
stration. The sales managers argued that the solution
would be to create a "one-stop-shop", a call-handling unit
which would take responsibility for all calls and answer
them immediately. In that way, they argued, the calls
would not be an interruption to the administrative work.
(An interesting assumption given that dealing with calls
did constitute a lot of the work. While it might be plausible to assume that administrators should simply process
papers, to do so currently required interactions between
sales and administration. This was a feature of the way
the system currently worked). The administration managers argued that a "one-stop-shop" was impractical and
that it would be better to use the established "experts" to
answer calls as they are the ones who knew the answers.
There was an impasse. Two strongly held opinions.*

As it happens, the administration department was registered
to ISO 9000. People worked to procedures. No-one had thought
to measure anything, to understand what was going on. What
was the volume of calls coming in? How predictable was it?
What types of calls came in and how predictable was each
type? How long (predictably) did it take to handle the different
types of calls? Were some more time-consuming than others?
How many of the calls coming in were calls which were caused
by a failure of the system which, in an ideal world, should be
eradicated? In other words, what can we learn about the predictability of demand and the predictability of response? And
what could we learn about the way the system responds? How
well does it respond to customers from the customers' point of
view and how efficiently does it respond to the various types of
demand? These are the data which would illuminate the
means for improvement; they tell us about what the system is
doing.

Without such data, management can only rely on opinion
to make decisions. In the above example, if the opinion of the

salespeople had prevailed, people in administration would look for evidence that it was the wrong thing to do (and vice-versa). The data required for informed decision-making were beyond the view of these managers. Managers measured staff activity in administration (transactions handled) and complaints; their preoccupation was to get staff to "do more" and "do better", whereas a systems view would have provided the means to achieve their end. Acting on the measures they had could only make things worse. If the managers had known what was predictable about demand and response, they could have agreed upon a new way of working against which they could have tested their assumptions. They would have been learning rather than trading opinions.

To work with the notion of predictability, managers need to know about the theory of variation. Deming compared ISO 9000 and the theory of variation in one of his last interviews (*Industry Week*, January 1994):

> *"ISO 9000, 9001, 9002 are conformance specifications — conform to requirements. But that's not enough; that won't do it. One must seek the nominal value of anything, what the best way is, not just pass the course. To meet specifications, do what is required — that is not enough. You have to do better than that. Achieve uniformity about the nominal value, best value. Shrink, shrink, shrink variation about the nominal value. That is where you get your payoff; that is where you get ahead."*

Managers have grown up in a world dominated by the ideas of "conformance to specifications" or "working to standards". Henry Ford showed the world what could be achieved by stan-dardisation. He reduced the cost of motor-vehicle manufacturing and, as a consequence, made motor transportation accessible to the mass market. Ford brought the world the benefits of mass production and it became the epitome of good management. The ideas spread from manufacturing to service organisations. Work could be managed if it is broken down into parts and those parts are measured for cost-effectiveness. The key to mass production was standardisation of parts and their assembly; no longer was there a need for fitters (workers who literally "fitted" parts by machining each to fit); manufacturing became assembly. The consequences of Ford's innovation are still evident today. Model T's in auction rooms often have components from different manufacturing years. One example can consist of parts which span thirty years of manufacturing history.

But standardisation is less than optimisation, as the Japanese were to discover. When work is made to a standard, variation remains. In assembled products, not all parts work together in exactly the same way. Variation in parts leads to exponentially increasing variation in the whole system, increasing the likelihood of failure. It was for this reason that the early motor manufacturing processes required huge "finishing" operations and, for example, early cars required drivers to be mechanics. Despite the overall improvements in automotive product quality, such differences still exist between manufacturers. Some manufacturers' finishing costs have been reported to be more than others' original manufacturing costs (see Womack et al., 1991).

Ko Yoshida calls working to standards "acceptability quality":

"If you are working on acceptability concepts, that is the quickest way to bankrupt your company" (Dr Yoshida, 1996 speech to the British Deming Association).

Standards are a compromise, but the idea of using standards is deeply ingrained in the traditional manager's psyche. They seek to protect a manufacturing process from only the extremes of variation. Components made to a standard are judged to be acceptable if they fall between acceptable limits (see figure 4.1). It was Taguchi who first showed the superiority of working to reduce variation. Rather than produce parts within acceptable limits — to a standard — he showed that it was far better to choose any point on the continuum (making this the nominal value) and make parts more and more alike As variation between parts is reduced, in whatever small amounts, the variation in the whole system reduces and thus decreases the likelihood of failure. In simple terms, this is why Japanese cars have become more and more reliable.

Figure 4.1

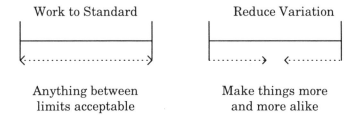

An American motor manufacturer opened a transmissions plant in Japan. After a few years, the American transmissions plant managers noticed that their Japanese counterparts were making transmissions which broke down a lot less (in fact, hardly ever). What action did they take? True to a red-blooded, competitive mentality, the Americans bought a transmission which had been manufactured by the Japanese. A co-operative response might have been to pick up the telephone and ask what they were doing.

The Americans took the Japanese transmission apart and measured its components. To their surprise, the components did not show the expected "tolerances" or variation. Perturbed, they sent their measuring equipment away for re-calibration, assuming it was faulty — they could have easily checked their equipment by taking one of their own transmissions from the line. There were no "tolerances" *(expected variations) in the Japanese transmission. The Japanese had been making their components "more and more alike", having understood Taguchi's work (the theory of the loss function).*

It is axiomatic that there will always be variation. No two tasks are the same, no two days are the same. Managers ignore variation at their peril. When people are required to work to standards the result is often demoralisation. If the standard is *within* the limits of "natural" (i.e. system-induced) variation (see figure 4.2), some days workers will be "winners" — they will meet or exceed the standard — and some days they will be "losers". It is inevitable because their performance is governed by variation in the system. It is management's task to understand and act on the causes of variation. Learning from variation is fundamental to continuous improvement.

Figure 4.2

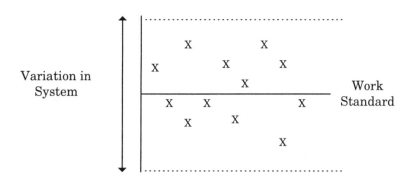

There are two types of variation, "common-cause" and "special-cause". In simple terms,* if measures taken over time are plotted in a control chart and all values fall between the upper and lower control limits, it can be said that all variation is due to

---

* This explanation is not strictly true but sufficient for our purposes here; for a more thorough explanation of interpreting control charts see Owen (1993) or Wheeler and Chambers (1986).

"common causes" (see figure 4.3). These are causes within the system; without action on the system we can expect performance to continue to be between the two limits on the control chart. The limits on a control chart, determined statistically, show what possible values can be expected to be produced by a process or system given the variation in observations taken over time. "Special-cause" variation describes observations which fall outside the control limits. They are due to a special event, possibly a "one-off". The value suggests that statistically this cannot be attributed to the same process or system — something extraordinary has happened.

Figure 4.3

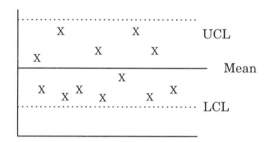

Common-cause Variation

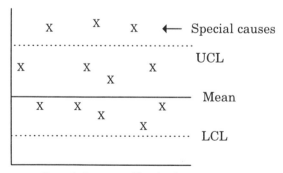

Special-cause Variation

The distinction between "common-cause" and "special-cause" helps managers avoid making decisions which make matters worse. In our experience the most common fault in management decision-making is reacting to a "signal" which is not there — in other words treating "common-cause" variation as though it is "special-cause". It is an understandable error. In real terms a number has gone up or down and the manager feels obliged to respond. But in practice his response might only increase variation; he might put in a new procedure or change a policy which only makes things worse.

In his famous four-day seminars, Deming would conduct what he called the red beads experiment. He would ask for volunteers ("willing workers"), show them their task and then allow them to perform a series of trials. The task was to take a paddle, which had fifty holes in it, and place it in a box containing mostly white beads and a few red ones. The object was to "get white beads", which of course was almost impossible because a few red ones would always creep in.

Deming would amuse his audience by behaving as a manager would. He would give a demonstration and make it the "work standard" — "If I can do it, so can you". He would repeatedly proclaim that the customer wanted white beads (and would tolerate just a few red ones, as achieved in the work standard). He would praise those workers who achieved the work standard or better — "Good work, you'll go far". He would punish those who fell below the standard — "Sloppy, try harder" and so on. After a training trial and a couple of work trials, Deming (as the boss) would sack those who had consistently under-performed ("We'll keep just the good workers — that way we'll get more of what we want"). Of course, in subsequent trials, some of the "good workers" also "failed".

It was a simple exercise with a profound point. People's performance is governed by their system. Nothing would change the fact that there were red beads in the system. It is the nature of "red beads" that they affect performance differently on different occasions.

To get an idea of the impact of "red beads" on performance, we often encourage managers to do as Deming did in his experiment — plot the performance of workers over time. In other words, make a control chart. If, as is so often the case, performance shows variation but is "in control" (i.e. predictable), then they can start working with their people on the causes of variation. To ignore the causes of variation (red beads) and to rate worker against worker (with no evidence to show that the differences are real) is a sure way to demoralise people.

A tele-marketing team was measured on number of calls, contacts, and "sends" (a sale subject to trial). Daily and weekly targets were set. Achieving target resulted in a bonus. Managers foolishly praised and paid those who made their target and "coached" or "paid attention to" those who did not. The people were demoralised. Roughly two days in any week they had to experience going home having failed to meet their target, yet they had been as busy as ever. They knew in their hearts they had done their best. However, their performance was governed by the system. Plotting performance on a control chart showed that their performance was predictable; differences were due to common-cause variation, there was little any individual could do to improve performance (see figure 4.4). On investigation it was revealed that the single largest cause of variation was the quality of the prospect lists. Lists had duplications, the remains of partially used lists were kept in people's drawers, stored for re-use when nothing else was available. As all lists came from the same source this resulted in waste. Customers were being re-called frequently (generating complaints), errors in the lists were being found more than once, some customers (at the back end of lists) would never get called. The second largest cause of variation was product knowledge, which varied extensively between operators. Other sources of variation were the time taken to process orders because some depended on other departments, the type of product, and the fact that there were frequent "fire-fighting" interruptions to the working day.

Figure 4.4

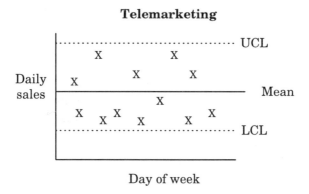

Telemarketing

People learned to do whatever they had to do to make their targets. They hid good quality lists, falsified activity records, "bounced" incoming customer calls to others so as not to get tied up with a customer problem and so on. They were not bad people, they were working in a bad system.

The performance of this system didn't depend on how the parts act independently (getting lists made "on time" and meeting activity targets for calls — the measures preoccupying managers), it depended on how the parts worked together. It is management's role to manage the interactions (or system), not to manage activity. Being clear about the purpose of the system and measuring performance in relation to purpose over time (to establish the extent of variation) are the first steps. Only attention to the causes of variation would result in improved performance. Improving the quality of lists, increasing the product knowledge of operators and removing the causes of customer problem-calls would improve the performance of this tele-marketing system. It is not unusual to find such "traditionally managed" tele-marketing systems under-performing by half.

Management of the tele-marketing team was focused on activity — the number of calls per person per day. These measures encouraged them to explain differences in performance as attributable to differences between people, hence the management job was thought of as "motivating" people — "get people to make more calls". The managers assumed people would be motivated by targets and bonuses, yet they presided over a system where the success of any particular call was beyond the control of their people. In these conditions people do whatever it takes to get the bonus, but they "know" they are at the mercy of the system. It is very demoralising to work under such conditions; the task loses its intrinsic value. Pride, the most important source of motivation, is lost.

Coming to terms with how the current system causes sub-optimisation is a powerful way of learning — it is important to learn why something is wrong as well as simply that it is wrong. Managers who rely on measures of activity to (mistakenly) manage productivity recognise the need to abandon them when they understand just how such measures are actually damaging productivity. They abandon them with confidence when they know which measures to use instead — that is, measures which relate to purpose — and they know how best to use them — that is, to learn from variation. ISO 9000 teaches managers nothing about this. If anything, it prevents such discussions even getting onto the table because of its approach to implementation (see chapter 7).

The capability of a process or system can be easily established by plotting its performance over time and determining, through statistical methods, what the process or system will predictably achieve while advancing, providing there are no substantive changes (see figure 4.5).

If a work standard is set at a level beyond the system or process capability (see figure 4.6), then nothing other than "cheating" will ensure that people avoid getting grief from their managers.

Figure 4.5

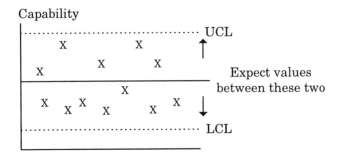

Figure 4.6

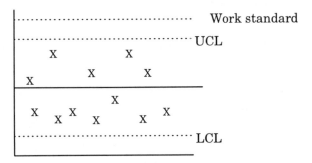

If a work standard is set at a level which is easily achieved by the process capability (see figure 4.7), there is no incentive to work for improvement; people slow down. In either case, the work ethic becomes "get to the standard", do whatever it takes to avoid negative consequences (being "paid attention to"). In human terms, this is no different from the experience of being "assessed" against ISO 9000. The anticipation of inspection of one's work by others will encourage anyone to do whatever they have to do to be seen to conform. In this way, ISO 9000 assessment, just like "management by the numbers", can cause distortion of a system or process, increasing variation —

people doing whatever is required to pass inspection (for instance, ensuring that the paperwork is up-to date, being seen to be applying unnecessary controls, hiding things) regardless of the impact on the service and efficiency of their business.

Figure 4.7

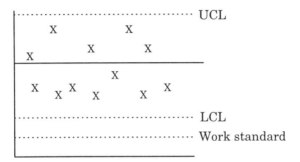

The principles associated with reducing variation apply equally to manufacturing and service organisations, but there are important differences as to how they should be applied, as we shall demonstrate.

"To gain customer trust, the variation of service must be reduced" (Ko Yoshida, 1996 speech to the British Deming Association).

Starting from this assertion, one can take either of two routes. The first would be to standardise service — the assumption being that customers' expectations will be managed by providing the same service anywhere in the world. The second route is to design the organisation to be customer-shaped — to respond to their particular need in a way which suits the particular circumstances. The question is: Who sets the "nominal value"?

The McDonald's fast-food restaurant chain is the classic example of the first route. The organisation has set the nominal value. But it does not follow that standardisation is always equivalent to excellent service. It was obvious to Ray Kroc, at that time a soft drinks salesman, that the McDonald's brothers' restaurant in Boston was a success. It was his idea to replicate the formula so that he could (as a supplier) do more business. The McDonald brothers gave him the right to franchise their idea and the rest, as they say, is history. That McDonald's has been a success is of no doubt, but it was an idea which was "tested" before being replicated — the evidence was that they had hit upon a "nominal value" that appealed to many.

However, there are many people who will not go into a McDonald's. McDonald's represents a standard offering that is the nominal value for many (but not all) people — they know it and they like it. Managers, seeing the success of McDonald's, argue for standardisation of service. We often hear international managers say they want their operations to have the same "look and feel" wherever they exist. It is more important to know what works — what matters to customers and how well you work in that regard. Indeed, it is vital to know what works before it is replicated across many sites, lest you replicate sub-optimisation. The replication of the McDonald's formula was not standardisation for standardisation's sake.

Service organisations differ from manufacturing organisations. Service is created at the moment of transaction. To apply Taguchi's thinking to service organisations requires a different way of thinking about his principle. It is the customer who sets the nominal value. The organisation should be designed to allow the customer to "pull value" from it at the point of transaction. Any departure from the customer's "nominal value" risks economic loss.

When the service organisation sets the nominal value it will increase the probability of economic loss. This is why service standards and guarantees have been a failure (to which we return in chapter 5). To take an example:

The customers of a country roadside restaurant may all have a different "nominal value". Fishermen, arriving at six in the morning will want service delivered differently from a family who arrive in the mid-afternoon. A businesswoman with a lap-top computer will have yet a different view of what would constitute good service for her. The managers of such organisations often mistakenly set work standards and procedures which effectively guarantee poor service to a high proportion of their customers. Typically, they specify how the customer should be greeted, seated and in what order things should happen. Any member of staff caught "breaking the rules" is subject to disciplinary action. A recipe for demoralisation.

Managers establish such systems because they believe it makes the organisation easy to manage. Management becomes specifying what people should do and checking that people are working to that way. The management tools are procedures and standards. Managers collect reports of activity (what people do) and pay attention to exceptions. They have no appreciation of the theory of variation. Moreover, they are unaware that their behaviour only serves to increase variation.

Management by procedures and standards has led to the rise of a new service called "mystery shopping". Mystery shopping is attractive to managers because it promises to give them data from which, they are told, they will be able to manage. A mystery shopper is someone who pretends to be a customer, visiting a retail outlet or calling a telephone service with a "tick-sheet" and recording the behaviour of the service agent. Managers are told that this data will be usable for improvement. Yet they cannot be; they only measure the mechanics of a transaction — did he or she smile, offer an alternative and so on. In practice, they can only be used to issue edicts and if the required behaviour increases variation, worsening performance, the managers never know. We recommend our clients to avoid wasting money on mystery shopping; we have found that mystery shopping always causes sub-optimisation of performance. Two examples:

> *In a telephone-based travel service, service agents had always been able to establish whether callers were bona fide members and thus entitled to the service. Non-members would politely be advised to try a good alternative for them. Managers employed mystery shoppers to "control" the behaviour of service agents. The agents would not dare deal with anyone who was not a member in their usual way just in case the caller was a mystery shopper. As a consequence, time to handle calls went up, productivity went down.*

> *A salesman in a car retailer picked up the telephone and perceptibly changed his demeanour. He sat down, took out a manual from his desk drawer and proceeded to deal with a lengthy conversation. On finishing we asked what had been going on. "That was a mystery shopper," we were told. "You can always tell, they ask questions that normal customers don't ask." He explained that the manufacturers used mystery shopping to determine a service score for retailers and that score would determine the retailer's bonus. In the time that he was on the telephone a number of potential customers went through his shop. It was economically more advantageous for him to deal with the mystery shopper than service customers.*

In every case we have studied we have found mystery shopping to be inhibiting performance. In one case we were surprised to hear that people liked mystery shopping but in fact they liked it only because it was their only form of feedback. They had fun "turning it on" for the mystery shopper and getting good scores on their report.

Mystery shopping finds a market amongst those managers who believe in standardisation. They see their job as determining what people should do at the point of service, issuing service standards, prescriptions and scripts. These things may or may not create value for customers, but in practice will always result in customer dissatisfaction at some level simply because the organisation has set the "nominal value". Customers want service to be customer-shaped.

Rather than specify service it is far better to ask: "what do we know about the predictability of demand and how does this system respond to demand?" Implicit in any demand is the "nominal value" — what the customer needs or wants and what would create value for the customer. The further the response is from the customer's need (variation), the greater the economic loss.

The compartmentalisation logic of "command and control" thinking is not limited to the design of organisation structures. A systems view of organisations shows the fallacy of conceptualising performance problems as people problems ("if only they would do it"). Failures in co-operation, poor morale and conflicts in our organisations are symptoms; they should not be considered separately from an understanding of the system. When they are, and are "treated" with training, the training usually does no more than treat the symptoms while the causes remain. Managers have been encouraged to think of the "human" (or "soft") issues as distinct from "hard" or "task" issues when the two would be better understood as interdependent. Empowerment is a preoccupation of "command and control" managers, but they fail to see that they have created systems which dis-empower people. It is only when a person's view of how to do work, how to understand it, control it and improve it changes that their behaviour changes. Changing the system begins with thinking differently.

ISO 9000 is not different thinking. It imparts a philosophy of controlling people's behaviour through procedures, forms and documentation. The assumption is that people need to be controlled. "Command and control" management thinking began with the separation of decision-making from doing. ISO 9000 was originally conceived when such doctrine was the norm — a norm which managers are only now beginning to question. ISO 9000 was a solution to problems which themselves were products of the same thinking — "why won't people do as they are told?" Controlling people's behaviour had, and continues to have, some success at tackling symptoms, but it fails to focus attention on the systemic causes — "why do people do as they do?"

Control of people's behaviour through procedures at best controls output, that is, by making output consistent (whether good or bad). This is why it is true to claim that an organisation can be registered to ISO 9000 and deliver poor quality (consistently). We do not argue that procedures are never helpful (although they are unhelpful in many circumstances); our argument is that starting from an attitude of "control" prevents managers taking the opportunity to learn and improve, as we shall see in each of the case studies (in chapter 5).

High performance organisations give control to the people who do the work — they are in control, not being controlled. The measures which are needed in such circumstances are not measures of conformance to procedures, or attainment of "traditional" output measures — for they afford no control, they only tell you what has happened. The measures required are those which illuminate what is going on in the system. In the examples we have used here the vital system measures were ones of demand and response. In order to learn, these measures need to be plotted in control charts, as understanding the predictability of demand or response and the nature and causes of variation would lead to learning and improvement.

One of the leading authors on learning organisations, Peter Senge, said that to look at the organisation as a system is to see two things: the scope for potential improvement — what it could look like — and the means or leverage for change. Changing the system usually means taking out things which have been limiting or damaging current performance. For example, removing activity measures, arbitrary targets or standards and ceasing to manage performance through budgets — in other words, changing structures, information and processes to enable the whole to better achieve its purpose. Managers will only take such radical action if and when they appreciate that their traditional means of control in fact give them less control: managing costs produces more costs. When managers understand their organisation as a system, the inappropriateness of traditional practices becomes stark. It is a major source of motivation for action. Action means "doing the right thing", putting in place the right system to ensure that performance is managed against purpose, and managed from a strong base of understanding.

In our experience, organisations registering to ISO 9000 show little such understanding of their current system, and the experience of registration only prevents them from taking such a view. In every organisation we have studied the first steps to registration were documenting procedures according to the prescription and creating a bureaucracy for their "management". The meaning of "continuous improvement" in such circumstances is no more than "improve through thinking of a better procedure": it is not a way of thinking which is underpinned by an understanding of the organisation as a system and how to manage through measuring and learning from variation. To manage an organisation as a system was and is a better solution. It is a view which is diametrically opposed to traditional "command and control" thinking; the view we took when we studied the cases which are the subject of our next chapter.

Chapter 5

ISO 9000 CASE STUDIES

In seeking to understand what ISO 9000 registration meant for organisation performance, we had learned that opinion surveys were unreliable. Those who had reported positive views were often unaware of the practical evidence to the contrary within their organisations. Examples of problems associated with ISO 9000 registration were everywhere. There were very few outside of the ISO 9000 movement who would heartily support ISO 9000 as a significant contribution to organisation performance; but we still knew little about what had happened in our organisations and on what scale. Was ISO 9000 contributing to performance in any respect and if so where and how? Were the much talked-of problems isolated or ubiquitous? Nobody knew. We needed to learn more about what would predictably happen to an organisation if it registered to ISO 9000. We needed to learn about cause and effect, so we turned to conducting case studies.

Our adversaries were swift to claim that case studies would not be representative. But we would ask the reader to consider the following argument: if one were to find examples of practice in organisations which were specifically linked to registration to ISO 9000, one could predict that others were likely to do the same. To be satisfied of the probability that others would do likewise, one would have to show how the practices were caused by the Standard (i.e. related to its clauses) and its associated system (i.e. the recommended method of implementation, the advice of assessors, marketplace coercion, managers who did not understand). If there is a predictive link we should expect to find that many of the problems associated with ISO 9000 registration are common to all registered organisations.

As we shall show, sub-optimisation associated with registration to ISO 9000 goes beyond the obvious problems of bureaucratisation. Organisations are making themselves less easy to do business with, often increasing their costs and, most important of all, as the management ideas associated with ISO 9000 gain acceptance as the "proper way" to do business, organisations are blinding themselves to the means by which they might otherwise improve.

Our purpose in conducting case studies was to understand what registration had meant in practice and how it affected performance. In the majority of the cases we report here the companies felt that ISO 9000 registration had been beneficial. While each of the cases is different, they show similarities in their approach. We will show that registration to ISO 9000, because of its implicit theory of quality and the way it is implemented, gives rise to common problems in its implementation. These are problems which damage economic performance and which also inhibit managers from ever learning about quality's potential role in improving productivity and competitive position.

TECH. CO.

". . . controlling sales and putting customers in their place"

Background

"Tech. Co." is a sales and distribution organisation based in the UK. All products sold by the company are manufactured by its parent company overseas. The products are high-technology products sold to business and government customers. Tech. Co. decided to register to ISO 9000 three years ago. The primary

reason for seeking registration was that Government customers were insisting on it. It was also felt that the company
might achieve some benefits from clarity of working procedures. Originally the company had seven divisions (organised
by product) and each division had its own sales order function.
It had recently centralised the sales order functions — in a
structural sense — but the people who worked within product
divisions still processed orders for the same products. The
primary change with centralisation was standardisation of
working procedures. Tech. Co. took advice from a consultant.
The work to first registration took three years and registration
was successful.

Registration to ISO 9000 meant the creation of nine manuals of procedures. One for each type of product, one called
quality and one for the warehouse. The manuals documented
what should be done at each stage of an order; nothing had
been left out. The quality manager took the view that sales
administration was now controlled. The standard procedures
meant that people would not get things wrong. He also viewed
salespeople as needing to be controlled: "They won't be able to
get away with giving administrators inadequate information
and what they provide has to be written down." He also saw
advantages in controlling customers: "Because we have controlled procedures we can prove to them what they have ordered if there is any dispute."

Has ISO 9000 Contributed to Performance?

The first operational problems were felt by sales. The attitude
presented to them by administration was that "nothing proceeds without the right paperwork". Furthermore, because of a
new procedure introduced to "comply" with ISO 9000 (see page
87), the warehouse would demand that directors "sign-off" returned goods before they could be made available as inventory.

There had been a cultural tradition of salespeople being
"heroes". They had treated "back office" staff work as drudgery, were always seeking last-minute changes to orders and

were rarely accurate with their form-filling. But now administration had been instructed to work exactly to procedures.
Some agreed with the quality manager that working to procedures would teach salespeople to pay more attention to putting
the right information on their paperwork, but sales behaviour
did not change. The same conflicts existed between sales and
administration; indeed, they were sometimes more acute because administration now had a specific stick with which to
beat them.

The causes of these conflicts were many, but the one cause
which appeared to be having the most influence was the complexity of pricing. Salespeople faced a variety of different circumstances when contracting with customers; the organisation
needed flexible administrative practices. The complexity of
current practices had been documented in the manuals. It
would be unlikely that an administrator would be familiar
with all situations and, furthermore, the manual would be unlikely to cover all situations (without being continually up-
dated). The consequences were an increasing sense of
"drudgery" amongst administrators and none of the original
problems were solved.

The sense of drudgery in administration was caused by the
way the new procedures had been introduced (it was said that
they were "dumped" on administrative staff with the directive:
"you are to work to these procedures"). The attitude in administration soon became "work to procedures" rather than serve
customers. Furthermore, it was a perspective which valued
working to procedures above finding and removing errors or
the causes of errors. When asked whether the new procedures
had improved performance, no-one could say. There had been
no collection of data on the performance of the administrative
practices prior to the new procedures and hence it was not
possible to determine whether things were better or worse.

The administration manager's attitude to customers ("the
procedures will enable us to prove what the customer ordered
if there is a dispute") was positively dangerous. What matters

when a customer disputes, or for any reason wants a change to an order, is that the need is dealt with promptly and courteously. The last thing the customer wants to hear is someone seeking to prove them wrong.

The thinking behind the new "goods returned" procedure was revealing. The volume of goods returned stayed at the same level as prior to registration (suggesting no change to the performance of the system). What did change was the way returned goods were handled. ISO 9000 has a requirement to control product which is returned by customers ("control of non-conforming product"). All goods returned by customers were now held in "quarantine", pending authorisation for release into the warehouse (for re-use). There had been considerable debate about what to do with returned product. Tech. Co.'s products were sensitive to excesses of temperature and light. If they had been subjected to adverse conditions while on the customers' premises they would be ruined. If product was tested on return it would be destroyed — the nature of the product precluded testing (or sampling) — any test would result in destruction. The choice was simple: return product to the warehouse or destroy it.

In the event, a compromise was developed. It was argued that product returned within fifteen days would be unlikely to have been subjected to adverse conditions. The procedure for returned product required the warehouse supervisor to check date of receipt against date of despatch and, where it fitted the new rule, to send a list of returned product to a director for signature. Signatories were hard to find. When they were available, they were not inclined to treat signing forms from the warehouse as their top priority.

But nobody asked "why is product being returned?" with a view to eradicating the problem. And, more interestingly, nobody had asked the question "have we ever had a problem with product being returned and then sent out on another order?" The answer, when asked, was "no". There had been no need to create this "quarantine" procedure. It would have been perfectly in order to place all returned goods in inventory. All of the available evidence showed that there was not a problem. Because of the Standard's requirement (control of non-conforming product) Tech. Co. had set up a procedure for an uncommon occurrence assuming it to be a common occurrence and had created a whole new set of problems. The result was losses to the system. At the time of this study, product to the value of half a million pounds was not available for sales.

If they had viewed their organisation as a system, and had measured the right things, they would have known that re-turned product had not shown signs of fault and would have recognised that customers in receipt of faulty goods were a rarity — when it did occur there was likely to be a "special cause" (see page 69). In the improbable event of a customer receiving faulty goods, the organisation could respond by en-gaging in excellent "repair" — give the customers whatever was necessary to solve their problem and create value for them. A good way to show what matters.

There is little that can be said in support of the view that ISO 9000 contributed to improving organisational performance in this case. It seems the implicit purpose of registration was to create a "control through procedures system", rather than help the business. It might have been labelled a "quality sys-tem" but its features were hardly promoting quality. The em-phasis on written work procedures was entirely unnecessary — a simple flow-chart would have been sufficient (and may have been of more use in clarifying purpose). The manuals produced for administration should not have been necessary. If they had a purpose at all they should have been used for job training. Used in the way they were only exacerbated the problems between sales and administration.

This was a classic "bomb factory" approach to ISO 9000 implementation. The purpose of this organisation is to distrib-ute product in the UK, that is, to sell. How should it do that, by what method? By creating value for customers, developing loyal customers, attending to customers' needs. Nothing was being done to understand and improve the core processes of achieving the organisation's purpose. ISO 9000 was making achievement of the purpose more difficult and more expensive. It had translated the organisation's purpose into "behave in accordance with procedures".

METAL CO.

". . . if you don't comply, we won't buy"

"Metal Co." is a supplier of processed metals to manufacturing organisations. Like many other organisations in the late 1980s, they were experiencing a high volume of questionnaires from customers wanting to know about their quality management system. The management felt that if they achieved registration to BS 5750 (as it was then), this would satisfy the various customer requirements.

Conscious of the dangers of over-bureaucratisation, the chief executive decided to appoint a quality manager, chosen because he had successfully taken two other companies through registration. The quality manager applied for assessment against the Standard immediately on appointment. He knew that there was a waiting period of about six months (because of demand) and he wanted to set clear expectations amongst Metal Co.'s employees. His recent experience had taught him that enthusiasm for the Standard easily waned. To quote him:

> *"I learned that if you give someone something to do and there is no value in it, they lose interest in it".*

There was no doubt in his mind, having been through the experience twice before, that the principle benefit of the Standard was, as he called it, "flag waving" — being able to show potential customers you were registered. We probed whether he really had such a jaundiced view and his response was:

"Behind the scenes the Standard is an inhibitor; if you follow the rules it slows you down".

He gave us examples:

"We had to demonstrate that instructions from sales to works were confirmed as correct. That meant the work instruction had to be signed. You were not allowed to have sales sign their own work, so works instructions would wait for signatures. To deal with the situation, people would 'cheat', they would simply take a bundle of instructions awaiting signature and sign them all."

You can imagine the impact on quality. A salesperson would, knowing that their work is to be checked by someone else, be inclined not to check it closely themselves. The person supposed to be checking would just sign them all off, assuming that the salespeople had done their job. No-one was responsible, responsibility was shared. It is easy to see how inspection produces errors.

"The amount of inspection required by the Standard was enormous. We had arguments with the assessors over 'final inspection'. Final inspection used to be the responsibility of the operator. Our process is quite simple: once a machine is set up, its performance shows minimal variation and all variation is always well within the specification. Hence inspection of the first and last piece made [by the operator] had always been satisfactory. The assessor wanted us to adopt a sampling plan, to sample pieces throughout the production run. There was no evidence that it was necessary, so we didn't — we just carried on as we always had but signed a form to say the work had been sampled. Furthermore, to do as the inspector had asked would have slowed production because you cannot inspect while the machines are running."

If he had followed the advice of his assessor and stopped the production run, it might have resulted in what Deming called "tampering": taking actions which increased variation and made the process less reliable. But the assessor has power and it is interesting to note how people deal with the power of the assessor — by giving up trying to fight it. Something else he said showed the peculiarity of the relationship between assessor and assessed:

> *"Our lead assessor told us ISO 9000 is difficult to achieve but impossible to lose".*

There was no doubt in his mind that the assessors meant that keeping the assessment was, from his point of view, the same as keeping the client. The assessor was just one component in the burden of being registered to ISO 9000:

> *"The most time-consuming and wasteful consequence of registration has been the growth in paperwork. The primary need for paperwork is to show that you have followed procedures. It is there to enable the assessor to do his job. How else can you show conformance, other than through records?"*

And the records required are pre-determined by what is written in the Standard. To take an example: the Standard requires documentary proof of the means by which the organisation approves suppliers. On an early assessment the assessor had discovered that Metal Co. had been buying materials from an organisation which it had not formally "approved" as a supplier. The purchases were low-grade raw material, suitable for a variety of applications where the finished product was not going to be used for external or "visible" components; the characteristics of the materials were in no way deleteriously affecting the final product. This, in the quality manager's words, is what their assessor told them they should do:

"He told us we should phone the customers whose supplies had included materials from these 'non-approved' suppliers and tell them so. Further, he said we should attach labels to all similar product leaving our premises to ensure that our customers knew their supplies were subject to non-approved raw materials."

Not only did this show a lack of common sense — the customers could not be adversely affected by the materials concerned — it showed a lack of commercial judgement. What did the assessor expect their customers to do in response to being sent such a warning? To avoid ever facing the same gruelling discussion about the extent to which this should matter, and to avoid ever having to upset customers in order to comply with the demands of an assessor, Metal Co. now pulls a list of suppliers off their purchasing database a week prior to assessment and presents this as the "approved supplier" list. It is a response to being "controlled" by their assessor; it does not reflect their attitude to working with suppliers. They are as determined as ever to work with their suppliers to improve quality, which brings us to the real value of this case study.

Much of what we have reported so far can be readily found in a host of ISO 9000 registered companies. It was when the investigation turned to working with suppliers and customers that particularly interesting issues began to emerge, issues which led to the inclusion of this case. To quote the quality manager, firstly on managing suppliers:

"To ensure supplier product meets requirements we have to take measures of all incoming product and plot it in SPC (statistical process control) charts. The suppliers have the same data but they won't release it to us because they feel it is 'company confidential'."

The consequence is waste; duplication of effort. More importantly, it is more likely to result in an adversarial relationship when discussing problems — "does my data agree with your data?" Suppliers who take the trouble to work with their customers learn more and improve their economic position. To understand just how profound this is, we have to move to Metal Co.'s customers, one group of which understands this thinking. To spare their blushes, we have omitted the customers' names from the following startling revelation:

"When supplying to (British automotive company), they wanted to know whether we were registered to ISO 9000, it was a mandatory condition of doing business with them. Having achieved registration, they were satisfied. Now they only come and talk to us when something goes wrong. When supplying to (Japanese automotive company), they had no interest in whether we were registered to ISO 9000 and from day one of being a supplier, they were in our factory working with us on how our processes worked to supply theirs."

The Japanese had an attitude of "work in partnership, learn, improve". It is win-win thinking. It reminds us of the following story:

A number of British organisations were competing to supply components to a Japanese manufacturer in the UK. Each had been asked to make a product according to a design. One had had a lot of problems and had been "back and forth" with trials, none of which had worked. It was this one which had won the contract. The managers were surprised to say the least, as nothing they had supplied had worked. When they asked why they had won the contract they were told it was because they had the right attitude.

And what, by implication, was the attitude of the British automotive manufacturers being supplied by Metal Co.? Contractual, hands-off, controlling, even coercive. The "big three"

American automotive manufacturers have taken this attitude one step further. Suppliers are being told that to do business they must be registered to QS 9000, a quality standard which goes further than ISO 9000 in that it specifies how the ISO 9000 clauses should be interpreted and evidenced in practice. As one American manufacturer is reported to have said, "if you don't comply, we don't buy". But are they buying quality?

This is what Metal Co.'s quality manager told us about his Japanese customers in the UK:

> *"They are not interested in ISO 9000, they are not inter-ested in your organisation as such; but what they do take enormous interest in is what you do to make whatever you are supplying to them. They work with you to understand your process; to understand how your process is affecting their process. They will send their people to help and they expect you to think and work in the same way. They are not 'soft' about it, they expect you to take it as seriously as they do."*

He followed his last point with a telling anecdote:

> *"We made a small change to a part we were supplying to them, we changed a lubrication oil. After a few months they raised questions with us which showed they had no-ticed a change in the product at the time we made it and had been exploring the reasons why but had been unable to find out. When we disclosed what we had done they were furious. To them it was natural to communicate all changes, they thought about the work in process terms."*

Metal Co. perceives their Japanese customers to have higher standards than their British customers, and their standards have nothing to do with ISO 9000. Yet the British and Ameri-can automotive manufacturers think they are being tough in insisting on registration to ISO 9000. The American motor manufacturers' drive to oblige their suppliers to register to the even more demanding QS 9000 is just "more of the same". We think they are foolish rather than tough. All the evidence points to the Japanese out-performing the Western motor manufacturers (see Womack et al., 1991). The difference is accounted for by attitude.

The difference starts with understanding and managing the organisation as a system. From this point of view, suppliers are part of the system, not merely "contractors". The Western manufacturers have realised, at least at a superficial level, that collaboration is important but their systems are designed to prevent it. The chief executive of Metal Co. illustrates the point:

"One of the American manufacturers held an impressive 'road-show' with European suppliers. As well as explaining their new world-wide structure, their message was one of co-operation and partnership with suppliers. However, in practice nothing has changed. Their buyers are targeted on reducing costs and this means they'll shop around and force down our margins. When we point out the inconsistency between their leader's message and their behaviour — for if nothing else they are ignoring the costs of taking material from a variety of sources — they make it quite clear that if we raise these issues with people 'above' them, they'll drop us from the suppliers' list."

His point is that efficiencies can be gained by working together, not by the strong coercing the weak. But the American manufacturer's system can do no more than the latter. It has been designed that way. It was not the buyer's fault that he behaved that way, that's how he is measured — he is a product of his system.

Metal Co. sees the same amongst its British customers. The chief executive again:

"Our British customers buy on price. If, for example, one has an order with us and then finds a cheaper source in the market-place, typically they will ask us to hold their finished order as inventory. The same happens if they buy from us in bulk; they achieve a lower price but we or they then hold inventory. In a number of different ways they play suppliers off against each other."

This is a problem of attitude. It serves neither party well to hold inventory. Neither is it simply an issue of cost. Many organisations embark on reduction of inventory to reduce cost. This is the wrong place to start, reflecting a traditional "command and control" view. When someone is "buying to budget", they will find it difficult to reduce the costs of the process. The paradox is that costs do fall as inventory falls, but the reduction of inventory is a consequence of working on quality. For example, achieving "batch sizes of one" or "single-piece flow" results in problems being identified immediately. It reduces waste. It improves learning.

Working to improve quality begins with understanding the organisation as a system. Co-operation follows. A system designed to improve quality would have roles designed to work between suppliers and customers (as the Japanese have), not roles designed to "optimise parts at the expense of the whole" (as the British and Americans have). Quality begins with a change in thinking.

To stay with Metal Co.'s sector:

The chief executive of a "first tier supplier" in the automotive sector had been proud to be the first to register to what was then BS 5750. His company was featured in a national newspaper in a major feature extolling the benefits of registration. We had kept a note of his name and by chance met with him some seven years later. He admitted that his company was like all others: that they had "done 5750" because they had to, that they rushed around to en-

sure that they would pass each audit and that it was a necessary condition of doing business in the UK. He also asserted that "clarifying procedures had been of benefit" but like others could not say how in any specific terms. When asked to feature in a national newspaper, he couldn't miss the opportunity it provided for publicity.

When we met he was proudly saying that his company was aiming to be "amongst the first" to register to QS 9000. We asked him what the differences were between ISO 9000 and QS 9000. He did not know. We asked him what he knew about Taguchi's work and the theory of variation. He knew nothing. We asked why QS 9000 was important to him. "An opportunity for flag-waving," was his answer. "We were the first in our sector to get BS 5750, we want to be the first with this."

Deming used to say that quality is made in the board room. He was right.

LASER CO.

". . . thinking we've done quality when in reality we haven't even started"

Background

"Laser Co." is a high-tech manufacturer, employing 150 people. Five years ago, a senior director (now the managing director) wanted greater "discipline" in the engineering function. Quality was chosen as a means. The quality manager wanted to introduce continuous improvement but needed a start and felt that ISO 9000 would provide the foundations.

The organisation has three main functions/divisions: manufacturing, engineering and sales. Engineering had a history of high staff turnover and it was felt that the "wheel was continually being reinvented" — the organisation did not retain any semblance of "how we did it last time". A further influence was that larger customers were starting to "make noises" about the need for a quality system. They were beginning to feel obliged to respond lest they should find themselves unable to tender for business.

Laser Co. took advice from a consultant. They found his advice "dogmatic". It was also found to be misleading — for example, the consultant told them that traceability was a requirement of the Standard. They agonised over this for six months. Eventually, re-reading the Standard, they discovered that traceability was only important if the customer required it; theirs did not. They soon learned to work on their own interpretation of the Standard and not rely on the consultant. They knew, as they went into the exercise, that they wanted to avoid too much bureaucracy.

Implementation

Manufacturing found implementation to be very easy. The personnel in manufacturing were all used to working in a structured way: they used work tickets, time sheets and had a structured management information system (MRP). The focus in manufacturing was on writing down what they did. As this was happening the quality manager had to stop people in manufacturing from improving things — as they documented their procedures, people found obvious things to change. He was concerned that people should actually write down what they did (initially without instant modification). Having got the more complete picture, he then encouraged review and improvements which were seized fairly eagerly. It is relevant to note the value that people get from clarifying their work procedures. Sometimes they are confronted with obvious things to change for the better. It makes one wonder what managers have been doing if they have not been doing that. Perhaps it shows how "attention to procedures" can be "bought" by managers as of palpable value and, hence, assumed to be "quality".

In engineering, implementation was more difficult. The prime purpose of introducing ISO 9000 into engineering was to establish a unified design process across the various groups. There was, prior to this, no predefined method. Furthermore, the personnel in these groups were used to working in fairly ill-defined environments. To a large extent this meant starting implementation from scratch. They reviewed, for example, the engineering change process. People learned just why the engineering change process had to be so involved — there were so many consequences stemming from engineering changes. With effort, implementation produced what was described as "remarkable" changes in engineering, mostly as a consequence of introducing procedures which would minimise the "reinventing of wheels".

Consistent with their desire to minimise bureaucracy, the implementation team dumped their procedures manuals in favour of flow-charts. It kept the processes in focus in a simple and meaningful way; they had learned the value and importance of "clarity".

At the end of our discussion, the quality manager expressed the view that the whole process had one essential driver — the need to improve efficiency in an environment of economic recession and headcount reductions. The whole effort took two-and-a-half years. Laser Co. claimed reductions in time, reductions in errors and reductions in waste. These were not quantified during our discussion. However, it is believable that such gains were achieved. It was through the endeavours of two managers that this progress had been effected. The two of them had to "make it happen". They felt it took a lot of "getting through to people"; the MD's interest waned at times (especially at end of quarter/year). Their view now, five years on, is that ISO 9000 is the foundation for other things to happen. They felt that without it, they would have been unable to get a company-wide focus for the quality effort.

Has ISO 9000 Contributed to Performance?

At the outset of this discussion, the efforts of the two people who behaved as "organisational entrepreneurs" — working across organisational barriers to make things happen — should be recognised. It requires commitment and effort to create change in organisations, usually due to fighting the current culture or *modus operandi*. The managers argued that ISO 9000 registration produced benefits. Processes were more clearly defined, resulting in less waste or more efficiency. They had recognised and sought to avoid unnecessary bureaucracy, and even went a further step away from the norm by getting rid of procedures, using flow-charts to provide clarity of focus.

Without doubt, this is a case where many of the usual excesses of ISO 9000 implementation had been avoided (excessive bureaucratisation and over-control through procedures). Should that lead us to declare it a success? ISO 9000, if it is to make a contribution, should improve economic performance, both internally in how the company works and externally with respect to the company's competitive position.

The extent to which ISO 9000 can or will improve economic performance will depend on features of the Standard (and their interpretation) and features of the company's current culture (or management thinking). For this case, we will first consider the impact of the current culture on performance.

This culture has various components, some of which we have learned directly from the case study and some that we can guess at from the clues we are given. Let us examine two:

Management by Attention to Output. During our discussion we learned that top management's attention "wavers from quality" at the end of financial periods. It is a sure sign that the company is run on output data. It will follow that departments have budgets, targets, variance reporting (difference from target, etc.) and it then follows that time will be given over to discussion, defending, promoting and surviving the "budget issues". Management works this way when it has no understanding of the concept of variation. Enormous quantities of time are given over to irrelevant and stressful activity. The company does not benefit, it loses. The managers leading this implementation had continuous improvement as their long-term goal. Continuous improvement starts from an understanding of variation — it is not an unending series of little "fixes" — and there was no measurement of variation anywhere in this system.

Work Methods. Manufacturing found ISO 9000 straightforward because the methods were similar to the methods in use; it is normal in manufacturing to have work instructions, job sheets and so on. By contrast, what is normal in high performance or World Class systems? One example works to four principles: single-piece flow, pull not push, control in the hands of operators (including the right to stop the line), and "automatic stops" on the line (if defective performance is automatically detected).

While Laser Co. had cut time for internal processes, the total order fulfilment time had not changed and appeared to be inefficient when "activity time" (the time worked on a product) was compared to "total time" (the time the product spent in their system).

Management by attention to process is a fundamental principle of World Class achievement. In Laser Co. the work methods were functionally designed and controlled and, by implication, there was no true process management.

Has ISO 9000 Helped?

The ISO 9000 advocates would say that it has and in this case, as with some others, we might have been persuaded to agree. After all, the organisation has gained clarity, improved efficiency and avoided some "common pitfalls". However, the avoidance of pitfalls is not a credit to ISO 9000, but to the two managers who implemented it. Gaining clarity and improving efficiency are essentially the same gains sought by the founders of this movement in the bomb factories. The result, then as now, is the control of output. But quality is not concerned with the control of output, it is concerned with improvement. Closer inspection of the way the organisation worked only raised doubts about ISO 9000's contribution to performance improvement.

What is most worrying is that the managers in this system might tell you that they have "done quality"; after all, they went through the steps as directed and achieved registration. How would this community respond if they were told there is an enormous amount still to do and it requires a fundamental re-think of current operating assumptions? This is a system which does not know what matters to its customers, and is therefore unable to turn such data into useful measures and shows no understanding of the importance and measurement of variation. This is not a quality system, it is a "command and control" system. It is bound to be sub-optimised. The chances are they would rationalise the current position — after all, they have "got ISO 9000" — and hence any real opportunity for performance improvement would be lost. And that is, perhaps, one tragedy associated with ISO 9000: people think they have "done quality" when in reality they haven't even started.

Quality methods are diametrically opposed to methods used in functional, "command and control" systems. This is a company which has avoided the worst of ISO 9000 and yet it has been unable to avoid the fact that ISO 9000 registration has led it to a place from which it will be difficult to influence more fundamental change. ISO 9000 has reinforced some aspects of "business as usual", but it has not been the start of a quality journey. Even more disturbing is the fact that this process took two years. A company of only 150 people, if they learned to act on their organisation as a system, should be able to make changes to improve economic performance in months, not years. ISO 9000 has decreased the probability that change will be possible in this case. If this seemed a good case of ISO 9000 registration, we can only hope their competitors are as complacent.

LAN CO.

". . . the nightmare assessor"

If Laser Co. would have been better served by knowing what mattered to its customers, "Lan Co." found out the hard way through registering to ISO 9000. Lan Co. is a network services company, providing its customers with networking solutions. In 1992 the owner decided he had to register to ISO 9000 as he did not want to be excluded from tenders. His customers were all Government, Health Authorities, Housing Associations and large industrial companies. As a consequence, all were requiring their suppliers to have ISO 9000.

Lan Co. took advantage of the DTI scheme, getting the services of a consultancy at a subsidised price for fifteen days. The consultant guided the owner, who had chosen to write the procedures himself. On each visit the consultant would outline how to approach each of the clauses and the owner would write the manual and associated documentation between visits. Having created the manual, procedures and work instructions, the owner brought in his installation crews to explain what ISO 9000 was about and what it meant for them. This was the first sign of trouble. Installation crews did not see the value of having to sign "as seen and understood" changes to work instructions; they were resistant to what they saw to be an affront to their common sense. Nevertheless, all installers were trained and the associated training records completed.

As it was a business which involved design, Lan Co. had become registered to ISO 9001. The owner remarked that it was not always perceived as an advantage. People would say to him that other companies were further ahead than him because they had ISO 9002! In fact ISO 9001 has more requirements than ISO 9002 in that it includes design control. But the real disadvantage of registration was to rear its head very quickly. The owner explained:

> *"Contract review became a major problem. We couldn't find a satisfactory way to suit our customers and suit the assessor. The Standard works fine if you go to site, prepare a set of drawings, agree what is to be done for the client and then nothing changes. But things do change, it is the nature of the business we are in. In many cases the clients change their mind, they make minor changes to equipment siting or requirements. Of course we respond — after all, we are a service business, but the trouble it caused with the assessors was unbelievable."*

We asked how many contracts were subject to change after acceptance — the answer was around 30 per cent. To continue:

> *"ISO 9000 required any change to be recorded. In simple terms this meant re-drawing or adding amendments to the specification and going through the process of agreeing the same with the customer. With large contracts that was fine but with small contracts it was totally inefficient."*

We asked how many of each the business typically dealt with in a year. His answer was about 5 large contracts, worth about 40 per cent of total revenue, and about 200 smaller contracts which accounted for about 60 per cent of revenue. The problem he had was that the assessors would specifically look for changes to the contract. He was unable to fulfil the requirements of the Standard as required by his assessors and remain in business, so he devised a "work-around": Every job had a "design control" form (according to the guidance of the assessor); if a change was required by the customer it was recorded on the design control document and the "all aspects clear" box ticked. The box was ticked regardless of whether the changes had been translated into additional drawings and "signed as accepted" by the customer, but now the owner was at risk of being "caught out" by his assessor.

The owner justified this course of action to himself:

"We are a service business. It is normal for customers to change their minds. Sometimes they want extra terminals, sometimes they want to change the location of PCs. Whatever they want is what we are there to provide. Most of these jobs were for hundreds of pounds, few were for more than two thousand pounds. The customers would expect us to listen to their needs and respond. They didn't value the design control procedure any more than we did. ISO 9000 was creating a monster which was serving no-one's needs except the assessor's. I would despair. One of our major customers was a Health Authority and I would say to myself we are not supplying a battleship. I was not being paid by the Authority for design changes and neither did it matter to the people whose PCs we were connecting that we did not stop work and re-write our work orders every time they changed their minds. In fact it was positively getting in the way of good relationships when we did. They were in a constant state of change. They wanted us to respond to their needs.

The assessor was keen to make hay on this issue. On one occasion during a customer site visit he cited the lack of customer verification of changes to an order as a non-conformance. The installation crews concerned knew that the customer didn't want to be hassled and there was no evidence of customers being in dispute or withholding payment because of contractual problems. But it was a problem for the assessor."

Lan Co. wanted to look after its customers' needs. Registration to ISO 9000 meant satisfying assessors over and above satisfying customers. Inevitably, Lan Co. learned that the only solution was to fiddle the paperwork to avoid hassle with the assessor.

"Assessment visits were always argumentative, it was as though their job was to catch you doing something wrong. The major fights were always over documentation. For example, if we changed a work procedure and failed to register that change in document control we were in for a 'right going over'. The slightest change to a procedure involved us in hours of work. If you changed a procedure you had to change the quality manual. In turn, these changes had to be recorded in document control. Then the new procedure had to be published and the people who would use that procedure in their work had to be informed. This required getting them together and having them sign a piece of paper to confirm that they had knowledge of the changes and then that had to be recorded as having happened. Such changes then required the recall and amendment of all of the quality manuals.

I found myself being tied to the office. The assessors assured me that if I got the management system working properly it would ensure that the organisation turned out a quality performance. It was a nightmare. I found myself becoming more and more detached from the business, knowing less and less about customers as I became embroiled in the paperwork created by ISO 9000. It was a method of management whose focus was procedures, documentation and control; it was not about customers and the people who provided service to them. For two years I stood in front of my staff telling them that this made sense, was necessary and was the same as everybody else was doing. But you can't ignore the obvious futility forever and the longer you do, the less your staff respect you.

In the days before ISO 9000, when a change was made to the way the organisation worked people were told about it. There were often changes because of the nature of the work; changes to software and hardware standards were frequent in a fast-moving area of technology. The culture of the organisation had changed from 'telling people', to 'telling people, writing about it, getting them to sign to indicate they had been told and then writing about that'. We knew this was silly, but it became a case of doing what had to be done to secure the contracts we were seeking.

I would dread the assessors coming in. They would claim they were interested in continuous improvement. They would go through the paperwork and check for details. For example design control forms were numbered. There were five people in the company who did quotes and they would give their work to a secretary for word processing. It was her job to type a draft and return it for final editing. When it was completed she would attach a design control form and give the job a number. All quotes would then go to my desk for final signature."

Who felt responsible? If the originator felt that the secretary would "sort out" any missing bits and she felt that others would, because they create them or sign them, it would introduce errors. Whenever more than one person is responsible, you get an increase in errors.

"From time to time the secretary would miss a number in the series. It would attract the attention of the assessor. He would want to know whether this was a job and was missing its paperwork or whether the secretary had made an error. In either case the assessor would record a non-conformance and would expect to see evidence of corrective action on his next visit. Typically, I had to write about what I had done to prevent re-occurrence, for example, conducting further training of the secretary."

Of course this was not a training problem — the assessor showed a failure to distinguish between common-cause and special-cause.

*"To avoid getting into grief with the assessor, I'd docu-
ment non-conformances I'd spotted which I couldn't correct in time — and almost all of these related to customer
contract issues — so that if the assessor spotted them I
could show that a non-conformance report was already in
the system. It became a game preventing them catching us
doing something 'wrong'."*

His antipathy to the assessor only grew:

*"Our assessors were to assess us for on-site accreditation.
On our first assessment the assessors were unable to assess on-site work because they had not yet achieved the
required registration as an assessing body. It made me
furious. Here was a company assessing mine which was
not itself accredited with the competence to do the work.
The consultants were quite relaxed about what I thought
was a glaring discrepancy. I could only recall all the pain
they had put me through on matters of contract review
and felt conned that they didn't have to pay the same regard to their dealings with clients."*

We asked what he thought "continuous improvement" meant
to the assessors:

*"Their attitude disappointed me. They never took an in-
terest in what we did. For them 'continuous improvement'
meant paperwork. They would go ever deeper into different parts of the business, I felt that they wanted to 'bash
every area'. After each visit from the assessors we would
have what we described as 'homework' — paper work to
do to correct the paper system. Things required changing,
cross referencing and updating. The assessors were incon-
sistent. Each would take a slightly different view of what
was important. Sometimes we would find ourselves telling an assessor that what he was asking us to do would*

overturn what his more senior colleague had instructed us to set up."

He learned how to deal with assessors:

"We used to cheat. We'd put things in the ladies toilet, safe in the knowledge that no assessor could find them (all assessors were male): spare parts which had come back from jobs, which the assessors would expect to be labelled; scraps of paper which staff might have used to work out a quote — the assessors would pick up such scraps and argue that the work was at risk of being lost and that there ought to be a form on which calculations were made; customer drawings which did not have numbers; all of these things would be hidden away to avoid grief. I'd get as many staff out of the office as possible: if the assessors couldn't ask them questions, they'd be less able to find things to criticise. The assessors view was 'You have to decide whether or not you want it' (ISO 9000). Their attitude was condescending. We put our procedures onto a computer. Immediately the assessor criticised us for allowing all staff to have access. They insisted that we create a password protection and we were obliged to give a copy of the password to one of the assessors who told us that he lodged it with their firm's accountant along with an instruction to open it only upon his death. It was like being in the secret service."

And what did ISO 9000 cost him?

"ISO 9000 registration cost us £50,000 in the first eighteen months, from start to first registration. I feel like it's the only time I have paid money to have a hard time. With the same money I could have invested in technical equipment and improved the service we offered to our customers."

But despite it all he had not given up on quality:

> *"We did a survey of our customers, asking them what*
> *mattered to them and how they found our services. What*
> *we learned was that ISO 9000 registration was irrelevant*
> *to the people who used our services. We learned that it*
> *was the purchasing departments who were demanding*
> *ISO 9000 registration of suppliers. We found that our cus-*
> *tomers were getting irritated with 'being chased for signa-*
> *tures' — something which was only occurring because of*
> *ISO 9000."*

Clearly ISO 9000 was making matters worse.

The owner of Lan Co. had other views of his experience with assessors:

> *"The assessors wanted installation engineers to carry*
> *their procedures manuals and up-to-date network stan-*
> *dards information. The latter were very expensive, it*
> *would have been economically impossible to maintain.*
> *Management review was a farce. Having had a discussion*
> *about what we were doing, we would find ourselves hav-*
> *ing to say, 'You know what we just talked about? Well*
> *now we're going to write the same and sign it.' It was like*
> *saying that people don't have brains and can't be trusted.*
> *One positive advantage was that you could always find*
> *the paperwork associated with a job if and when it was*
> *needed in the future. Not a high frequency occurrence, but*
> *valuable nevertheless."*

Some benefit in comparison to the sub-optimisation he was experiencing. The assessors had forced a production view of the world on him. He needed something to help him develop his service view.

SYSTEMS CO.

"... is ISO 9000 a good starting place?"

"Systems Co." is an engineering services organisation which manufactures handling systems and installs the same on customer sites. The customers use the systems in their manufacturing and packaging operations. Systems Co. has been registered to ISO 9000 for a number of years. To achieve initial registration, Systems Co. sought the help of an accredited assessment body. Having interviewed several, they chose one which they felt demonstrated the least "bureaucratic" attitude and showed the most desire to be helpful and constructive in the relationship.

In this case, we followed a routine surveillance audit being conducted by the firm of outside assessors. As the assessor worked we kept an interest in two questions: what is he looking for and why? The second question leads to a corollary: does this help improve the system? The assumption is that this would tell us about how the auditor (and client) think of the Standard and how their thinking relates to quality issues in the organisation.

Prior to our meeting, the client informed us that the auditor was "one of the better ones". We took this to mean that he would take a view of the organisation as a business system rather than be pedantic about (his) interpretation of the Standard. We had been told that the auditor's organisation had "recognised that their market has shifted to a focus on things which had benefit to the business". The client saw the audit process as one of "support and assistance" to the business.

In this routine surveillance (described as a "health check" by the auditor), the auditor focused on several "mandatory" issues and then selected three areas of the business. The purpose of the audit was to raise any items of non-conformance which, if found, would be given an agreed date for resolution.

The mandatory issues were:

- **Changes to personnel**. We probed why. We were told that change to a significant position (for example, the chief executive) would require investigation as to whether this could adversely impact the quality system. The criteria for choosing whether to investigate such changes were specified in a manual produced by the assessing organisation's quality system.

  To summarise the discussion which ensued: If the chief executive were to change, how could an auditor determine whether to record what he sees as a non-conformance? It seems the auditor would seek evidence of the new leader's commitment to the quality system through words and deeds. It seems to us that this is a method which relies on anecdote and interpretation. What chief executive would not assert that he or she was "up for quality"? Would chairing quality reviews be sufficient to be evidence that he or she was doing things in support of the quality system? A judgement must be made; yet any decision could only be based on the auditor's view of the world.

- **Changes to equipment**. This follows the same logic as the above to the extent that the auditor takes a view on what equipment changes should be subject to review.

- **Changes to the documented management system**. Any changes should be reviewed to ensure they are consistent with the requirements of the Standard. Once again, decisions are based on the auditor's view of his own quality system, the client's quality system and, above all, his view of the application of the Standard.

- **Results and corrective actions from internal audits**. It is relevant to note that at the time of first registration the client had established a group of internal auditors (according to advice from the original consultants). The group has since been disbanded. When the current chief executive was appointed he charged the quality manager with changing the way quality was working away from "quality control" and towards prevention. He took the view that control should be in the hands of people doing the work. It is also relevant to note that the chief executive has subsequently charged the quality manager with reducing the documented quality system from two manuals to fifteen pages.

- **Feedback from customers**. Complaints, returns and any corrective actions. Again, this relies on the auditor's interpretation (for example, whether problems should be treated as "special-cause" or "common-cause").

- **Management review**. To stand back and determine the effectiveness of the quality system. Again, this is subject to interpretation by the auditor — what might be the auditor's mental model of the purpose and mechanics of the management review?

- **Use of the assessor's logo**. Apparently, the assessing organisation was implementing a directive from the UK Accreditation Service which dictated requirements for the proper use of "quality badges" on stationery and the like. In this case the issue was irrelevant, the chief executive had already decided that he saw no value in "advertising for the assessor".

The three areas of the business the auditor inspected in detail were engineering, manufacturing and customer service.

Engineering

In engineering, he examined in detail an enquiry file. The file records customer information and he was interested in how the system made sure the customer got what was expected: how drawings were numbered, how you would know you were working on the right drawing, that the right information went to the right places and how, if changes were made, they were accommodated.

The auditor followed the progress of a file through to manufacturing. He was interested in how the jobs "came in", how the system tracked changes, and how work was planned through the manufacturing resources.

This is "bomb factory" quality — adherence to procedures. It seems plausible that work should be tidy, orderly and accurate. It is "just in case" thinking. It does have merit and can, in some circumstances, be of value but it is essentially a means of control. It really has little to do with quality. In bomb factories it dealt with the immediate problem, it controlled output. It is indeed plausible, even reasonable, to presume that the control of drawings, changes and relevant customer information will help ensure that the customer gets what the customer wants. It clearly could affect quality if these things went wrong and were not repaired before something reached the customer. But if we are controlling these things it should be because we have *demonstrated* their influence over the quality of output, not on the basis of "just in case". We should instead question whether the right things are being controlled.

Why did the organisation develop this "control of activity" approach to quality? Because they had learned it from their consultants and auditors. Even though they are cutting back on it, it is still the principle means of quality control — and all it can do is control output. It should be termed management control, not quality control.

Quality is concerned with improvement. Improvement requires action on the system. In this case the only action on the system encouraged by the introduction of ISO 9000 was auditing for non-conformance and the management review. The system was assumed to be in control if people behaved according to procedures. However, these procedures do not necessarily relate to what matters to customers, and subsequently may or may not tell us more about the performance of a process.

It is fundamental to quality thinking that measures (and controls) should be related to purpose. What is the purpose of this system? If it is to be a quality organisation, the measures in use should tell us how well it works and whether things are improving. This system had no data concerning what mattered to customers. There were customer surveys, but the items were written internally so it was impossible to determine if they understood what mattered to their customers. If they had known, they might have been able to turn "what mattered" into internal operational measures to track action for improvement. To take two possible examples: how often do they deliver assembled product on time as originally committed? There was no data readily available (and in use), although everybody estimated 75 per cent. How often can the engineers complete their work on-site without recourse to manufacturing for something which should have been foreseen? There was no data; estimates ranged from hardly ever to nearly always.

Manufacturing

In manufacturing the manager used measures of labour hours. The purpose was to charge hours to jobs. It is not an unusual measure: many organisations do this. The assumption is that improving utilisation of the labour force will improve efficiency, hence lowering costs. The manager's task is to ensure that jobs keep to budget. This is the classic problem of "budget management": the starting number is a reasonable guess from the contracting department, and any variation between the starting number and the final number could be due to a variety of causes. Minor variations are ignored, major variations are reported although there is no evidence of whether these are common-cause or special-cause and, in any event, the starting number was a "guess". If major variations are acted upon, what can the manager do? The likelihood is that any action will result in distortion of the system, the priority being to "be seen to come in on budget", so the manager might shift labour around to suit budgets not customers. The managers told us that "no distortion of data or other dishonest actions occurred here" and that may be so. The point is it's more likely that they will. More importantly, this is the type of data which

could be dangerous if used to drive a "get costs down" understanding of improvement.

Improvement starts with understanding what matters to
customers. The data which might help learning and improvement (thus reducing costs down *and* improving service) was
not in use: how predictable is our delivery versus first commitment? How often are engineers able to fit the customers'
equipment without returning for something which should have
been catered for? What are the type and frequency of customer
and engineer demands on the organisation?

In this, the manufacturing side of the organisation, the prevailing attitudes were more in tune with the implicit attitude
of the Standard. People placed a high value on having the correct procedures and the right documentation ("doing things
right" rather than "doing the right thing"). When we discussed
some of the features of the system which, if understood, might
lead to improvement, the general response reflected an assumption that these things were normal. But there was no
good data, only opinions.

Customer Service

Customer service was the auditor's final area to audit and it is
fair to say that he said something which surprised us. The
auditor was interested in the organisation's approach to customer service. What this meant was:

- whether the organisation had determined how often to
  conduct customer surveys

- how the results of such surveys were being built back
  into the management system

- how the organisation knew what mattered to its customers.

It was the last item which surprised us. Having seen so many
organisations (including this one) dwelling on control of the
customer's order and because of the emphasis placed on this by

the "contract review" clause of the Standard, it was a nice surprise to hear an auditor emphasise that "what mattered to the customer" mattered.

However, the auditor was primarily concerned to relate customer survey data to the management system. He assumed that "what mattered to customers" was being measured by the customer satisfaction survey. Indeed, it is typical of many organisations that vast quantities of customer satisfaction surveys are used, but with little understanding of what matters. His line of thought was concerned with "corrective" actions as defined by the management system (as written) and their reporting. The chief executive preferred to see the data as something which would drive action in the relevant part of the business, without a formal management decision-structure over it (he subscribes to the view that action is of more value than reports). This approach was characteristic of the changes the chief executive had made to the way the organisation worked.

It would have been of greater value to the organisation if the auditor had focused on the methods employed to gather customer data and the development and use of related measures to improve performance. For example, interviews with customers showed that they wanted quotations when they requested them (not within a period). The contracting department took immediate action by controlling this with the use of a white-board: customers' desired dates for quotations were written up for all to see, which improved performance immediately: they had acted on what mattered to their customers. The use of a white-board would make this procedure difficult to audit — this auditor did not comment but many others might have. As an aside, with all documented procedures (which by definition exist to be audited), it is worth asking whether the documentation is only in place so that the auditor can do his job. That is to say, the procedures provide no operational value to the organisation and may even detract value. When you discover such procedures and find that they are in place at the insistence of the auditor, you start to wonder just how wide-spread these problems are.

It had also been noticed that 75 per cent of all quotations work resulted in no order. It was a healthy perspective to take, the sort of view a systems-thinker would take. The department had started doing work on understanding the causes, but this work had, so far, not included data from customers. But it was typical of the way things were working in the more progressive parts of the organisation — people had the right (systems) perspective and only needed help (if any) with method.

When we asked how people were measured in the contracting department, we were told there were no individual performance measures. We regarded this as a good response. Typically in such departments one finds "activity measures" used in such a way as to undermine performance. The measures in use in contracting related to purpose (quotation on-time as committed, revenue); the use of these will be more likely to contribute to a climate of improvement. In other parts of the organisation, more traditional attitudes prevailed. It is not to suggest that people differed in their commitment and potential contribution. Our experience has taught us just how much behaviour is conditioned by features of the organisation which we call system conditions.

Had ISO 9000 Been Beneficial?

The quality manager would claim so. He would argue (as do others) that ISO 9000 was a good starting place for the quality journey.

There is no doubt that clarity (of procedures) is an aid to good performance. But if with clarity comes unnecessary documentation and inappropriate controls, has it been beneficial? This organisation has spent the last three years drawing back from and eradicating dysfunctional aspects of registration to ISO 9000. Should this be regarded as a necessary cost? Surely not. It was argued that ISO 9000 gave the organisation the impetus. Wouldn't it have been more beneficial to allow the customers to be the impetus? If so, wouldn't the organisation have moved more quickly along the road of discovering the right methods and measures to improve performance?

Systems Co. is an organisation which is learning to behave as a "customer-driven system". Yet was this learning facilitated or hindered by registration to ISO 9000? It could only have been hindered. ISO 9000 registration had focused on documentation of, and adherence to, procedures. There was no evidence (other than anecdotal) as to the consequences on performance.

UTILITY CO.

". . . standards mean worse service"

Privatisation of our utility companies has been accompanied by their regulation: monopoly suppliers must be controlled against abusing their position. The regulators are people of their time; they seek to impose conditions or constraints on the regulated, and to do so they employ thinking which is current and to them, no doubt, plausible. As we shall see, this has resulted in the accommodation of ISO 9000 as a preferred means of control, and it is having a destructive affect on the performance of utility companies.

The Electricity Regulator has published "Best Practice Standards". The regulator is concerned to ensure that information about customer service standards is reliable and consistent over time and between companies. It seems a reasonable thing to establish and it suggests that we will be able to learn and improve. In giving Regional Electricity Companies (RECs) guidance about how to achieve this aim, the Regulator states: "The requirements are similar to those specified in ISO 9000." The regulator believes that if an REC has ISO 9000, it will meet the requirements of "best practice".

The Regulator expects RECs to establish and publish service standards, and then to report breaches of these standards in such a way as to allow audits and reviews to be conducted. The procedures must cover how "breaches" are identified, recorded, reviewed and reported. The reporting system must include structure charts, job descriptions, training records and a defined process for reporting. This whole effort should have an appointed representative and should be documented. The levels of documentation required are specified and changes or any document control should also be defined and documented. All "failures to conform" to the documented system have to be recorded and subject to corrective action and, finally, the whole system should be subjected to internal and external audits. It is easy to see how the Regulator thinks that ISO 9000 will cover all of the requirements.

What happens in practice? Firstly, the RECs produce service standards and send them to their customers. It seems to us that very few people will read these leaflets; none of us has and when we ask others we find few who have and those few usually cannot remember the contents. The standards are entirely arbitrary, they are not set with an understanding of the REC's capability. Some examples of our own REC's guarantees:

"If your main fuse fails, we will arrive within four hours of your call. If we take longer, we will give you 20 pounds."

"If your supply fails due to a problem with our system, we will restore it within twenty-four hours of first becoming aware of the situation (excepting exceptional circumstances). If we don't succeed and you let us know within a month, we'll give you 40 pounds (100 pounds for business customers)."

"If you are concerned about your meter, we will reply to you within five working days or visit your home within ten working days. If we take longer we will pay you 20 pounds."

And so on they go. It seems to us that customers don't want guarantees, they want service. They don't want recompense, they want action. As we shall see, the action caused by these standards is undermining performance. Some examples:

> *One Regional Electricity Company (REC) is reported to have set up a method to avoid failing on guarantees for appointments; if they know they are going to fail to meet a guarantee, they phone the customer to re-arrange the appointment. In this way it is not recorded and reported as a failure.*

This is normal behaviour when people are subject to arbitrary controls (see Seddon, 1992). The ingenuity of people becomes engaged in fighting the system. It results in distortion, demoralisation and, hence, sub-optimisation:

> *If the person who made the appointment is not the customer as defined by the name on the bill (for example, wife, husband, son, daughter, neighbour, etc.), any failure to keep an appointment is not regarded as a failure because the commitment was not made to the "lawful" customer.*

The contractual thinking implicit in ISO 9000 is given full rein, as is the thinking about procedures and people:

> *Failures are recorded on a form which requires the name of the "person responsible". Failure forms create fear. They also ask "what action was taken by the manager in respect of the person responsible"?*

It is assumed that all failures should result in action to prevent re-occurrence; a failure to understand the distinction between "special cause" and "common cause" (see page 69). Action on every failure will inevitably lead to increased variation and less control; it will make performance worse.

Managers of these organisations are heard to say that "heads will roll" if there is a failure on service guarantees; as a result, their staff become preoccupied with covering up failure. The consequence is that the only thing that can be guaranteed is that the Regulator will get unreliable data. Perhaps their response, as they discover this, will be to tighten controls. If it is, it will be evidence that they are not learning either. The Regulator is afflicted by the same thinking as the ISO 9000 fraternity. To believe that work should be defined, controlled, documented and audited is to make work less efficient and less attractive to customers.

> *A repair crew arrived at a customer's house late in the evening. The customer's supply was down and the crew were about to dig up the garden. The customer would have been happy for the crew to start in the morning but to do so would have been to fail to meet their service standard. The crew did as they should (to meet the need of the customer) and mis-reported the incident to avoid attention from their managers.*

When a customer telephones or writes to their REC, they want a response to the problem, not an acknowledgement in a specified number of days. Customers are less interested in filling in forms to get recompense than seeing their REC work on improving the quality of service delivered. The "standards system" is not capable of being used for improvement and will causes a rise in complaints and bad "word of mouth". The measures required for improvement lie elsewhere.

Service standards are assumed to make service better. The Government Minister for the Citizen's Charter put it this way:

> *"The way to improve service is to set a standard, publish performance and give people the means to complain when performance is not to standard."*

He could not be more wrong. When you set a standard (with no understanding of what current performance is predictably achieving) a host of problems occur. When the standard is below current performance, people slow down, they work "to the standard". When the standard is unachievable in terms of current performance, people do whatever they can to avoid being caught or "fail". There are many examples of these phenomena occurring throughout public and private sector organisations. People are not learning and improving their work, they are doing whatever it takes to avoid remonstration.

One consequence is that published data are always unreliable or "distorted". League tables do not motivate or teach, they only de-motivate. "Standards" thinking also adds to costs — now we have bureaucracies of standards setters, procedures writers, internal and external auditors and complaint handlers. Complaints are rising. We could have spent the same money solving the problems.

If, for example, the RECs knew more about the predictability of customer demand on their system and the predictability of their current response, they would be in a position to start work on improvement. We will explore how these simple ideas would have resulted in a far better solution for these and other organisations in our next chapter.

What Can We Learn from the Case Studies?

Any of these cases — and every other case of ISO 9000 registration we have researched, could have made great strides in improving quality and performance, and could have done so in a much shorter time than was devoted to ISO 9000. Some were more grossly off the point than others. To see their opportunities for improvement the managers of these organisations would have needed to take a different view, a view which the ISO 9000 experience had prevented them seeing. Worse still, ISO 9000 registration led many of these managers to assume they had "done quality" (or service) when, as we have said before, nothing could be further from the truth.

The cases are not exciting examples of positive change. Despite seeking them for the last five years, we have yet to find **any** exciting changes associated with ISO 9000. There is nothing to enthuse about and plenty to question. Not only was little achieved in those which might be argued to be the best cases of ISO 9000 registration, but some have clearly taken a step backwards. We have also seen how registration to ISO 9000 involved considerable time and resources — resources which might have been employed in a better way.

Are these cases unusual or unrepresentative? Not in our experience. As we stated at the outset, every organisation we have worked in which is registered to ISO 9000 shows evidence of activity which is damaging economic performance and is present because of the perceived requirements of the Standard. We have yet to find an organisation which is registered to ISO 9000 which does not show such evidence. Given the nature of the thinking implicit in the Standard and promulgated by the assessors, we predict that any organisation registered to ISO 9000 would have evidence of sub-optimisation, through the establishment of inappropriate activity — "doing things right", according to the Standard — and/or through lost opportunity — not doing the "right thing", according to the needs of customers and the business.

To those who would maintain that these cases are unrepresentative, we would ask: How many cases do we need to confirm or deny the proposition that ISO 9000 is damaging economic performance? How many more cases would be necessary to establish that we have a serious problem? Furthermore, we have sought "good examples" of ISO 9000 registration from our many correspondents and have yet to find one which did not show sub-optimisation attributable to ISO 9000. We are confident that what we have discussed here is representative of the experience of registering to ISO 9000 — indeed, we have discussed our observations with hundreds of managers and have yet to find one who would refute that they are representative of the general experience. ISO 9000 registration leads to the types of consequences reported here because of its inherent theory of quality. There is a better way.

Chapter 6

THERE IS A BETTER WAY

The better way begins with understanding the organisation as a system. When working with managers who are leading change in their organisations, we have found it helpful to make distinctions between "command and control" thinking and "systems" thinking. To distinguish the two helps them clarify what to do "instead", and reinforces the point that quality is not "extra work". It is a different and more beneficial attitude towards working. When embarking on change, managers have to learn to give up doing things which they had regarded as good management and gain new skills. We characterise this mental and behavioural shift as a transformation (for that is what is needed) from "command and control" thinking to "systems" thinking (see figure on following page).

A Better Perspective

"Make and sell" is a fundamental tradition in command and control management thinking. It is to think "push" rather than "pull". Factories build products, marketing and sales sell them. There are always arguments concerning whether and how well the decisions about what is produced are based on customer needs. "Pull" thinking, on the other hand, assumes it is better to make to order; to ensure the customer "pulls" value from the system. It cuts time, inventory and waste; "pull" results in improved quality.

	Command and Control Thinking	*Systems Thinking*
Perspective	Top-down hierarchy, functional procedures	Outside-in, process and "flow"
Attitude to Customers	Contractual	What matters?
Decision-making	Separated from work	Integrated with work
Measurement	Output, targets, standards: related to budget	Capability, variation: related to purpose
Attitude to Suppliers	Contractual	Co-operative
Ethos	Control	Learning

Laser Co. was an example of the traditional manufacturing attitude. They could have made great strides by changing to a "pull" system. ISO 9000 serves to maintain a "make" or "push" view of manufacturing. The Standard asks: *"by what procedures is production controlled?"* A better question would be *"how does the system manage demand and flow?"* Systems Co. was closer to "pull" thinking: they assembled to order. But the organisation still showed a traditional manufacturing attitude: they had no measures which related to how well they responded to demand — the first step in managing flow. All the measures in use related to costs. Attention to costs suboptimises performance. Managers become concerned with "making their numbers" at the expense of the system. The real costs are in the system — delays, duplication, errors, time, materials and so on — and most of these don't show up on management accounts. Management accounts do have limited value. They tell you what has happened, but they don't tell you what is going to happen. It might be logical to assume that if every function makes its budget, the organisation is performing well. But if managers are using budgetary measures to manage, they will be ignorant of the causes of costs and might easily take action which makes things worse.

"Management by the numbers" is the most common expression of this attitude. The same attitude — "define and do" — is evident towards other features of work. In Tech Co. we saw how procedures became more important than purpose. Not only did this make things worse for the customer, it also damaged morale. In Metal Co. we saw how following the rules (procedures) slowed down work. Laser Co. illustrated how the logic of procedures fits with a traditional view of manufacturing. Here is another example:

> *We studied a lift factory which was registered to ISO 9000. We found it was spending half a million pounds a year re-fitting lifts which didn't fit first time on site. More than that, they found five out of six lifts to have faults when assembled in the factory prior to shipping (a wasteful activity in itself). Everything worked to procedures but no-one was learning; the means were obscured by the value placed on ISO 9000. There were plenty of procedures for dealing with non-conformance, none for how to learn.*

The lift factory consumed more than forty per cent of its revenue in waste — profits were poured down the drain. Emphasis on procedures was the wrong focus — it was a system which predictably produced waste and reported the same between functions (allocating blame).

While the managers at Laser Co. fought the excessive dogmatism of their ISO 9000 consultant, they nevertheless subscribed to the same traditional (functional) view. It is a view which results in documentation of how things "should" be done, when perhaps we first should be questioning why and how well things are done. It is true that in their case improvements were made through clarifying procedures. As we have said several times clarity is extremely important — peo-

ple need to know what their job is and why they are doing it —
but clarity doesn't have to come with encumbrances (bureaucracy and verification). Laser Co. will not improve from their
current position without establishing operational measures
derived from what matters to their customers; their focus
should be value and flow. This is more than flow-charting (a
useful step beyond writing procedures); it is determining the
"value stream" — the specific actions required to travel from
an order through to finished product in the hands of a customer — and cutting out all waste (for example, time, materials and errors).

All traditionally managed manufacturing operations show
large quantities of waste when viewed as a "flow" or "value
stream". The same problems are apparent in most of our service organisations: work is typically designed and managed as
functional specialisms in the mistaken belief that optimising
the parts — which usually means controlling costs — will optimise the whole. An example:

> *Customers experiencing a fault on their computer equip-*
> *ment contact a call centre. The call centre's job is to log*
> *the call. The call is passed (as an electronic record) to the*
> *diagnostics function whose job it is to call the customer*
> *back and determine the nature of the fault (is it hard-*
> *ware, software, application, network, etc.). Having made*
> *a decision the diagnostics group pass the call to the speci-*
> *fied "expert" group who, effectively, cover the diagnostic*
> *work again and take remedial action. When one looks at*
> *the "value stream" — the work required to be done to solve*
> *a problem — and compares it with what happened to*
> *each call, there is abundant waste and duplication.*
> *What's more, the whole system only gets it "right first*
> *time" for 30 per cent of the calls.*

By understanding more about the nature of incoming calls
(what types and how predictable?), they were able to move the

decision-making to the front end of this system, where customers called in. It improved service and productivity immediately.

A systems view of organisations leads to a different collection of problems to address. Managers who learn to take a systems view give up their preoccupation with budgetary or output data, management of activity and procedures and, most of all, they give up the idea of the division of "decision-making" (management's job) from "doing" (the worker's job). Instead, they work on the "causes of costs" — the way their system works to deliver what matters to their customers — and the means required to control and improve performance. It is an outside-in and "flow" view of the organisation instead of a top-down and "functional" view. From this point of view, the many conditions which have inhibited performance improvement (ISO 9000 being just one) become evident. Managers are faced with the task of removing the old ways of managing at the same time as introducing the new. This is not as daunting as it first appears, but it does require a different set of behaviours from managers. Remote, "by the numbers" management is replaced by hands-on, "value-flow" management. Leadership is, after all, the engine of change.

A Better Attitude to Customers

ISO 9000 declares that it is intended for use where:

> ". . . a contract between two parties requires demonstration of a supplier's capability to control the processes that determine the acceptability of product supplied."

Managers need to question whether a "contract between two parties" should be the focus for their relationship with customers. Perhaps it had some relevance for the provision of bombs in World War Two, perhaps it was the only way to establish basic contractual controls over the performance of companies building power stations and the like. But a contractual relationship differs from a service, partnering or co-operative relationship. As we saw with Metal Co., the opportunities for partnering with customers (and suppliers) were lost through an obsession with contractual thinking. ISO 9000 is part of the current business-to-business relationship, contributing to a way of working which hinders mutual performance improvement. The work to be done to improve "joint processes" starts from a different attitude, but co-operation is less likely to occur in a contractual atmosphere.

In a similar way, ISO 9000 has caused organisations who supply directly to consumers to miss the point. How many of these customers require organisations to demonstrate anything other than *to be of service*? Customers want service to be "shaped" according to their demand, pure and simple. And if it is poor service, if it doesn't fit with or exceed their expectation, regardless of the reason, they will vote with their feet. There have been countless surveys which have shown that more than 70 per cent of customers who take their custom elsewhere do so because of a bad service experience. In Lan Co. we saw how Contract Review increased the probability of a bad service experience. In Metal Co. we saw how the assessor explicitly advised action which would damage the relationship with the customer by unnecessary, over-bureaucratic emphasis on supplier control. In Tech Co. we saw how the Standard led to administrative attitudes which were defensive when dealing with customers — "we can prove what you ordered". Furthermore, it engendered greater conflict within their own company — "nothing moves without the right paperwork".

The Standard declares that the requirements are aimed at *"preventing non-conformity"*. In 1994 this was changed to say that the standard's requirements are aimed at *"achieving customer satisfaction by preventing non-conformity"*. It begs the question whether customer satisfaction is determined by *conformity*. Customers' views of an organisation are made up from the various transactions they experience. "Conformity" thinking is a relic of "contractual, manufacturing" thinking; it is only concerned with production as defined. The customers' concerns go beyond it. This is why organisations can be rated as having poor quality service yet be registered to ISO 9000. If a product or service is poor, it is of no value to declare that it is consistent or that it conforms with what has been designed.

What was striking about the case studies — and in our experience is all-too-common in British organisations — is that with the exception of one department in one of the organisations, they had no idea what mattered to their customers, the starting point of a systems view. The exception was System Co.'s quotations department who were delivering quotations at the time customers wanted them rather than to a standard. It is true that some of the cases (including Systems Co.) did customer surveys, but we have learned to treat customer surveys with extreme caution. Most often customer surveys focus on "how was it for you"; they do not tell us much about "what matters", and it is what matters which should drive the design of products and services. World Class organisations are designed in such a way as to enable customers to "pull value" from them rather than "battle hard" to get what they want and then be expected to give a view on how it felt. The "how was it for you" type of customer survey hoodwinks managers into believing they are learning when they are not — learning starts by knowing what matters and how well an organisation responds to what matters. Systems Co. had been registered to ISO 9000 for a considerable time and had only just begun working on what mattered to their customers; it could have and should have been their first action. If understanding what mattered had been established for every point of transaction (not just quotations), and that had been followed by establishing internal, operational measures which illuminated how well they responded, they would have been able to improve performance.

The Standard had not encouraged these organisations to find out what mattered to their customers. Rather than facilitating improvement, Contract Review was a hindrance. It held up orders in Metal Co., it upset customers in Lan Co., it was translated into service standards — a major cause of waste — in Utility Co. Contract Review has been responsible for many of our service organisations becoming worse at providing service. But it is the foundation for all that follows: the Standard requires an organisation to *"establish and maintain documented procedures for contract review"*. We are not warned of the risk of translating this in such a way that makes things worse for and, hence, loses customers.

Metal Co. showed evidence of what appeared to matter to their customers — a plethora of surveys asking about their quality management system. Like others, they were spurred into ISO 9000 registration by the fear of what might happen if they did not comply. There is little doubt that registration is not what actually mattered. These surveys were being generated by people who felt obliged to do as expected by their quality management system as defined — the blind were coercing the blind. Some refer to this phenomenon as the "ISO 9000 chain letter". It is the purchasing clause which has given rise to this allegation.

In the service sector, Contract Review has resulted in actions which make it more difficult for customers to get service. The 1994 review of the Standard placed even greater emphasis on this type of thinking. The Standard now requires definition and documentation of requirements before the submission of a tender and it requires any verbal orders to be *"agreed"* (implying documented, otherwise the assessor cannot determine that it has been agreed) before their acceptance. The result is a proliferation of forms requiring signatures before the customers get service. Bureaucracy has become a part of the service experience; consequently, the service experience has worsened. Furthermore, you find customers having to "work" the organisation to get what they want. Managers have decided what people "should do" in their various functions and, by implication, have decided what customers should expect when they transact with each function. It is the other side of "preventing non-conformity": decide what conformity is, what people should do. Many service organisations have been designed from this point of view. An example from a correspondent will illustrate the problem:

> *"I received an offer from a well-known credit card company. The essence of it was that, as a managing director of a company, they had chosen me as someone who should be a card-holder; they said they would not put me through hurdles as I was already "qualified"; and all I had to do was sign a form and they'd issue me with a company card. I thought 'great, I've heard so much about how good their service is and I'd like to try it for myself'. The card arrived. Then I realised that I had done something silly. I use another card for this business (the one they obviously got from a mailing list) and if I had thought about it, I should have asked for the new card to be put on my second business (a relatively new business, for which I needed a card). Being busy I just left it, not bothering to call (as asked) to 'activate' my card.*
>
> *Late one evening in the office, one of their people rang me. He was a personable young man. I was glad he called. I told him why I had not called to 'activate' and he said it would not be a problem, my card could be changed. Being very happy, I listened as he took me through what was obviously a script, the relevance of which I could not see (nothing they couldn't have told me before or later and had no bearing on the purpose of the call as I saw it). But I put up with the script because I was happy, I was going to get my problem solved. Then came my first shock. At the end of his script the young man told me I should ring another number to solve my problem. I was not impressed and told him so. I told him what motivated me to become a customer in the first place. He assured me that I could expect better going forward. I rang the number and got my second shock — an IVR machine. Of course I had to*

wait to the end to get the code for accessing a person and when I did so I got music. I waited for an interminable time, got through and was then told I had to fax this request to another number. My third shock. I gave up. Not happy. This should have been easy."

Reflect on this organisation. Was the young man being measured on the number of validations he did? He did not want the customer's need to get in his way; his managers were obviously not attuned to customer demands which went beyond what they had designed at this point of contact, other than perhaps issuing procedures instructing that these demands should be routed elsewhere (by the customer taking action). What did these managers know about the extent of calls which were outside of the intent they had designed and what plans might they have had to redesign this service to make it better for the customer? Did they even think this way?

Had the managers responsible for the call-centre justified the IVR machine on the basis of costs and productivity? Had they used anything more than traditional cost accounting to argue cost/benefit? What had been the impact of this innovation on the customer? How was such data gathered? Was it usable for decision-making? To the extent that this organisation exemplifies traditional, "command and control" managerial precepts, their system will be sub-optimised. Is this why they are marketing to people like our correspondent? Are they losing customers? If they are, it is easy to see why.

When organisations are designed this way, customers are implicitly expected to be content being dealt with according to the activities prescribed (by managers). Work is prescribed and measured. The "ISO 9000 view" is to assume that any non-conformance will be detected and "managed". However, a non-conformance in ISO 9000 terms is likely to be thought of as an operator doing something wrong — failing to follow a procedure. The more important "non-conformance" is the failure of the system to respond to a customer demand — these failures will only show up as complaints, yet most customers will not bother to complain, they'll just walk away.

As we have stressed, quality is not about control of non-conformance, it is about improvement. That it is a requirement to establish and maintain a documented system is questionable for any organisation whose customers have no need for them to demonstrate anything more than providing products or services which create value. Indeed, rather than what matters to customers, all the evidence suggests it is "what matters to assessors" that is driving ISO 9000 implementation. And what matters to assessors is much the same as what appears to matter to the committee re-writing ISO 9000 (see page 39); their efforts are engaged in maintaining the status quo.

The advocates of ISO 9000 argue that adherence to procedures assures control. This is to assume that control of procedures will ensure no variation in performance. However, there are always many sources of variation. When you look at an organisation from the customers' point of view (outside-in), it is easy to see how control of procedures will always increase variation (and thus worsen control). Why? Because customers' demands are customer-shaped, not necessarily procedures-shaped. And if an organisation is not customer-shaped it will inevitably take longer to deal with certain demands, deal with them less efficiently and get more complaints. The 1994 review of ISO 9000 resulted in the requirements for handling complaints being re-stated more specifically: *"procedures for corrective action"* should include *"customer complaints and product non-conformities"*. Further, it says that these should be investigated and the results of the investigations *"recorded"*, corrective actions taken and new controls applied to *"ensure that corrective action is taken"*. This creates an increase in the bureaucracy for managing complaints which will add to costs, maintain complaints and probably cause other forms of sub-optimisation (unnecessary procedures, increased inspection, delays to the work-flow).

The language of the Standard encourages managers to think about complaints in terms of documentation and corrective action: corrective action could apply to *"non-conforming product, work processes, customer complaints"* and so on, and should result in *"preventative action"* which should be recorded if changes to work procedures are effected. In this way, all non-conformances are treated as though they are "common-cause", as if they are predictable and caused by the system, and action is taken to prevent re-occurrence. The result is, potentially, a proliferation of procedures which may have been unnecessary. If the event was in fact a "special cause", a "one-off", a new control would now delay the whole system. The Standard says nothing about how to determine what sort of problem is occurring (common-cause or special-cause) and how one might then go about preventative action. The failure to distinguish between "common-cause" and "special-cause" variation is usually manifest as "just-in-case" thinking. The returned goods example from Tech Co. is an extreme example of it and, as we saw, it is not a good idea to proceduralise something which is unpredictable. The same error has been institutionalised in some larger organisations through document control on their IT systems — the electronic complaint procedure obliges the worker to treat "special causes" as though they are "common causes" and thus establish new procedures (through *corrective actions*) which only worsens the situation.

The 1994 review went on to say more about *"preventative action"* than had been said previously. *"Procedures for preventative action"* are to include *"appropriate sources of information"* and examples are given: work process, audit results, quality records, service reports — all examples which may lead the investigator down the wrong path if they know nothing about the theory of variation (and note that managers in the organisations studied would talk of processes, but had yet to establish the means to manage their processes).

The focus on complaints is the wrong focus. A better attitude to customers starts with knowing what matters to them and turning the same into operational measures. How else could one improve in the eyes of one's customers?

A Better Way of Decision-making

What we saw in the case studies was that the "command and control" mentality of our current management mind-set was attracted to the idea that work should be controlled by creating, documenting and inspecting procedures. In Systems Co., this meant inspection of their procedures as defined (in functions). This is not the same as understanding how well they worked; improvement needed different thinking and different data. If they had worked on how well their processes delivered what mattered to customers and had employed capability data, showing how well they achieved it, instead of relying on financial (cost) data, they would have had the means to learn how to improve — they could have made better decisions. As a corollary, if these better measures had been in the hands of people doing the work, their workforce could have been making decisions — learning and continuously improving service to their customers. Instead, the same headaches were experienced by the engineers, all problems of "design" not coinciding with "delivery". It is a perennial problem of traditional, functional, cost-based decision-making.

Decision-making in the thinking of the Standard centres around "do we do as we say we do?". In organisations which have been designed as functional hierarchies, registration to ISO 9000 "locks in" the waste by making it "invisible"; probably the most compelling reason to give up ISO 9000. What *is* visible becomes the focus of decision-making; it is defined by what is written about in manuals of procedures. It is the stuff of the inspector's work. The focus becomes meeting the requirements of inspection, not understanding and improving performance. As we saw in Metal Co., this results in unnecessary inspection and decisions about requirements for inspection being made by the assessor. It is no surprise that people object to their assessor's view of requirements; sometimes they just do not make good sense. In Lan Co. we saw how the assessor was argumentative, despite the fact that Lan Co.'s customers were suffering from the excesses of his strictures. He took an attitude of "catching them doing something wrong", which led in turn to the owner getting his people out of the way when the assessor was coming, something we have had reported to us by many correspondents. People can't be "found out" if they are not there.

Being "found out" is akin to being managed by "attention to output", the primary means of decision-making in "command and control" organisations. In all of the case studies and in most organisations we work with, management by "output data" is the norm, the order of the day. The problem is that attention to output inhibits learning. It only encourages people to do what they have to do to "meet the number" or "pass the assessment". We also observed how this phenomenon distorted the measurement and reporting of service standards in Utility Co. People had to do whatever they could to avoid getting grief from management and management sought to avoid grief from the regulator. If, for each of the customer transactions defined as service "guarantees", they had known their capability — what they currently predictably achieve — and had set to work on the causes of variation, people might have been motivated, contributing and learning. As it was, people were demoralised and the system was not improving. It could not improve; the means for improvement were out of the hands of management. If the utility companies are to be obliged to report to regulators, they would be far better off reporting their capability and investing their efforts and resources on improving it. Their current system (guarantees, refunds and associated reporting bureaucracy) is all additional cost and cannot be considered a foundation for improvement. To know how to improve would require measures of capability and work on the causes of waste and variation. The choice of measures should be driven by what matters to customers, and that is unlikely to be "having to fill in forms and receive financial compensation" when things go wrong.

In the language of the Standard, process management is not about establishing capability and learning from variation; the clause concerning what the Standard calls *process control* requires an organisation to *identify and plan* the work that it does. It is at the heart of the philosophy behind ISO 9000. Work should be planned and then controlled according to the plan (that is, non-conformance detected and prevented). It appears plausible, but it is at the root of the problem. Organisations and managers assume, a priori, that the right way (of working) can be decided, a priori, whether by managers or the people doing the work. It is a far more effective strategy to assume that the first step in quality improvement is to understand how well the process works currently, before documenting or controlling anything. The ISO 9000 requirements for "planning" relate to those processes *which directly affect quality* and the purpose is to ensure that such processes *are carried out in controlled conditions*. An understandable (if limiting) sentiment if you are making bombs, but an approach which values control over learning — learning starts with how and how well — and thus causes a failure to learn and improve performance.

Exposing the thinking behind its origins, the Standard places great emphasis on inspection and testing throughout the production process — it is a production view of the organisation, a "pass/fail" decision. Many studies have shown that inspection only increases errors (and more inspection means more errors) yet it has been a further requirement of the Standard that inspection should be *carried out by personnel independent of those having direct responsibility for the work*. This is a throw-back to the Standard's origins. It assumes that people cannot be trusted to control and improve their own work (which would result in less errors). In the 1994 review, the emphasis on independent inspection was rendered less explicit. However, just in case anyone wanted to take the risk of having their people "inspect" themselves, the ways in which people are able to take responsibility has to be defined and documented, such that they go through *designated channels,* and the requirement for personnel to conduct *verification* (inspection) remains. The whole philosophy of quality by inspection is based on the assumption that decision-making should be separated from work. It is diametrically opposed to quality by making improvement through giving control to operators and learning how to reduce variation — the latter philosophy of quality empowers the individual, the former does not.

Probably the single biggest influence on the bureaucratisation associated with ISO 9000, the clause on document control, requires organisations to *establish and maintain procedures to control all documents and data that relate to the requirements* (of the Standard). The 1994 review extended this requirement to include documents of external origin. Furthermore, the Standard requires a bureaucracy for documenting any changes to procedures and a bureaucracy for conducting reviews of procedures. Finally, a "master list" of the documentation is required. No wonder, when confronted with the consequences of these obligations, people question whether these requirements are doing anything to improve performance in the organisation or simply enabling the external assessors to do their job.

ISO 9000 is an artefact of command and control thinking. It ensures that what is written into the quality system is a philosophy of control and inspection; decision-making is separated from work. It is an approach which leads to decisions focused on whether people work as planned — not whether the system is being managed for improvement.

One correspondent put it this way:

"After five years of ISO 9000 I have come to the view that it is about compliance, not quality. It doesn't really drive improvement. We thought we needed consistency to get

improvement started and maybe we did but ISO 9000 made us look at consistency and conformity, variance from what should have happened was treated as important. We now know it would have been more useful to learn from variation, something we discovered only recently. ISO 9000 has been de-motivational. It is not about 'faster, more efficiency, trying things' and so on, it is about 'do it this way and record failure'. It's like getting a bad report at school."

This is the entry point — its the first thing managers focus on — what do we have to write down to satisfy the assessor? Managers would be far better off addressing a different question: how well does it work at the moment? If these organisations had understood what mattered to their customers and turned the same into operational measures, they could have established ways of working which would have resulted in improvement. But that is not the way ISO 9000 registration happens. Taking a systems view would be a better place to start.

A Better Way of Measurement

Measures should be derived from purpose. In Tech Co. the purpose of the organisation was to sell and deliver products to customers. Knowing how well they did this (capability) and how predictably they worked (variation) would have been a better starting-place for improvement than controlling people's behaviour through procedures. Similarly, Systems Co. should have been concerned with measures of their ability to ship and fit what the customers wanted without experiencing failures. Measures derived from purpose help managers to focus their action on the system.

Improvement is achieved through re-designing the way the process works or reducing variation. Managers who have no idea of the theory of variation should take a set of numbers they often use for decision-making and put them into a control chart.* If managers accept the theory of variation — that a system or process can be expected to produce values between the upper and lower limits unless something extraordinary happens — the first thing they usually learn (in our experience of "command and control" organisations) is that the process is stable but it shows wide variation. When you know that you can expect to get values at any point between the upper and lower control limits, and too many values at the lower end would put you way under budget, it makes you stop and think. The variation in values is caused by the system, not the people. Clearly there is no point in shouting at people. It is a compelling argument for finding out more about the system.

Sometimes wide variation in measures of a system is caused by the measure being representative of a number of processes. For example, sales data might relate to a number of sales processes. So it is helpful to obtain data for each of the processes, which should be considered separately. In many organisations obtaining data of this sort takes a little time, demonstrating how removed they are from sources of data for improvement. It is also frequently the case that management actions ("paying attention to output") cause widening variation — people pull data forwards or backwards to be seen to "meet their numbers". They comply with work standards or targets regardless of the impact on service, efficiency or revenue. When managers see the consequences of their decisions through seeing data over time it can have a profound effect on the way they subsequently think and manage. Measures of variation help managers decide whether a process should be re-designed or continually improved (they often need both, a number of times).

Utility Co. showed just how damaging the whole idea of work standards can be when they are translated into customer service guarantees. The "Contract Review" mentality was evi-

---

* Resources for calculating control charts are identified in the Recommended Reading.

dent — "we tell you what we will do and you have means of redress if we don't do it" — and the consequences for the organisation and customers were devastating. It is an object lesson to all who believe that service standards are a good thing. Standards are anathema to quality, they always cause suboptimisation. Guarantees and other forms of work standards appear attractive because they give managers something to "manage". They are similar numbers to the usual functional budget numbers and are reported in similar ways (this week versus last week). In each of the case studies we saw how managers were "used to" managing with output data (activity and budgets) and setting standards or targets. Few realise how managing this way causes sub-optimisation.

Better measures start with a different view. Take, for example, Laser Co.: using measures of time — a process measure — might have had a profound impact on quality and service. At the very least, this would have alerted management to the difference between activity time (the time taken to make a product in the "value stream") and the total time products spent in the organisation. But managers don't usually look for these things. They are preoccupied with functional measures such as measures of activity; it appears to them that more activity must result in more productivity. This is not true. We work to the general principle that when we find managers managing activity we will always find sub-optimisation as a consequence (for examples, see pages 71 onwards); rarely have we found evidence to the contrary. ISO 9000 reinforces this thinking; things that can be measured (activity) can be managed. It is not the way to improve performance. To improve performance you need measures of capability and variation in relation to what matters to customers. They lead to better decisions. It is the same thinking which informs how best to work with suppliers.

A Better Attitude to Suppliers

For the first fifteen years the purchasing clause required organisations to select sub-contractors on the basis of their *ability to meet sub-contract requirements, including quality requirements* — it reminds us of the plumber, reported in a national newspaper, who was reported as using his friend as a
sub-contractor "because he's good" but who was found to be
non-conformant by his assessor because the assessor wanted
documentary proof. The plumber could not get over the idea
that he had to write down that "Joe" would be used as a sub-
contractor "because he was good". In the 1994 review, the purchasing clause was extended to emphasise the evaluation of
suppliers in respect of their *quality system and any specific
quality assurance requirements;* increasing the probability that
organisations will do the easy thing and insist all suppliers are
registered to ISO 9000, regardless of the impact on performance.

The proliferation of supplier assessment questionnaires has
continued. One crazy example:

> *In 1992 we published a book called "I Want You to
> Cheat". People in organisations bought the book and thus
> we appeared on "supplier lists". Once our company name
> became visible to someone responsible for exercising the
> purchasing clause of ISO 9000, we would be sent a sup-
> plier questionnaire asking us about our quality system.
> All for having sold a book to someone in the organisation
> for £7.95.*

Suppliers usually regard such questionnaires as a threat — in
our case it was just funny — but the most common consequence is that people feel they ought to do whatever it takes to
get registered. As we have shown, coercion is unlikely to establish learning and improvement. Instead it fosters
"cheating", people do anything to avoid being found out and —
fear of fears — risk losing registration (despite the fact that

there is no evidence to suggest that organisations lose out if they de-register.

Metal Co. showed how they "cheated" to prevent the assessor "catching them out" using a "non-authorised" supplier. Where they thought the evaluation of suppliers to be important they acted, but in practice, as we saw, they were actually having to "control" supplier product because suppliers were nervous about publishing their quality data. A competitive rather than co-operative attitude.

It was interesting to note the different attitudes to quality between Metal Co.'s customers. The British saw ISO 9000 as an entry point, whereas the Japanese began the relationship by working on common processes and were indifferent to ISO 9000. Which behaviour reflected a better understanding of and approach to quality? Metal Co. could have made great strides for improvement if they had been working co-operatively with their suppliers and customers. ISO 9000 reinforced an alternative, "contractual" regime. In their case, increased inventory was an obvious symptom, adding costs throughout the value chain and hampering flow.

One might argue that sectors such as civil engineering and munitions supply need contracts between supplier and customer. The construction sector has trumpeted the need for change from its contractual, adversarial relations for the last ten years. But it is a sector whose system is designed to maintain adversarial behaviour between contracting parties: there are armies of independent professionals who earn money from "squeezing" suppliers against the terms of their contracts. The gains made by the independent professionals and the extra costs borne by both parties are all costs to the system. A quality approach would be to work together for mutual benefit. Contractual thinking begets adversarial relations; in turn, this prevents learning. ISO 9000 has the wrong ethos.

The Resultant Ethos

The Standard's ethos is to assume, a priori, that documentation and control of people's behaviour in procedures will prevent problems. Yet there is no evidence to support this view. It is a control ethos, not an improvement ethos. It further assumes that you can't trust people — staff or customers. A focus on procedures leads to people behaving in ways which value procedures over purpose (whether they like it or not). It is easy to see how ISO 9000 registration can lead to demoralisation and a deficit in learning.

The ethos we need is not what should we do, but how can we learn? Improvement starts with being prepared to change thinking. When organisations are run on "command and control" principles, the numbers in use do not easily facilitate learning; they tell you more about what has happened than what is happening and why. Worse, the data in use usually cause sub-optimisation: people work to make their numbers or standards at the expense of the system. Taking a systems view shows the extent to which command and control management causes sub-optimisation. It is a powerful source of motivation for change.

An improvement ethos starts with "what matters to customers?" From there we would need to learn about how well the current system responds to "what matters" — and to what extent the current response is predictable. It is to look outside-in, and from that perspective seek to understand what is happening predictably with respect to "demand" and "response". How well do we deliver product or service according to what matters to the customers, how well do we respond to the various demands they make on our system? How predictable are the demands customers make and what causes them? What are the things that we currently do that help or hinder our performance? Taking a systems view leads to improvement.

Understanding the causes of failure — why we fail to meet customer expectations — is one way of introducing managers to the fundamentals of systems thinking. If you know that your performance is lousy and you learn why, you are in a far better position to improve performance than you were if you were relying on the usual output data ("driving by looking through the rear-view mirror") — at least you know what is going on and you can predict what will happen next week if you do nothing to change it. When you can see how much waste is caused by your organisation's own actions you can also see how to stem the causes. The case for action becomes self-evident. Understanding the organisation's capability with respect to both what matters to customers and what is important to the organisation (efficiency and revenue) generates the urgency and focus for improvement.

> *A professional services organisation with 55 branches was being assailed with complaints by a major customer for the inaccuracy of their work. In desperation they decided to set up a central team to check all the work, which meant all branches submitting their work to Head Office rather than directly to the customer. Quality improved only slightly; more than 50 per cent of the work showed errors and many errors still 'got through' the Head Office net. Top management had been attracted by the notion of ISO 9000, believing that consistency was their problem ("it would work fine if everybody did as they should") and that was what the Standard was aimed at. It was also considered advantageous from a marketing point of view to be registered to ISO 9000.*
>
> *An ISO 9000 consultant was shown their problem and he agreed that it was grist to the ISO 9000 mill. His recommendation was to review the procedural material and establish clear responsibilities for what was to be done at each step in the procedures and how the work should be checked. Quite sensibly, the consultant advised an analysis of errors to identify the most common and to ensure that the new procedures were written to be as "idiot proof" as possible with these errors in mind. A central team was*

*established to write procedures based on the customer re-
quirements. They started work by tracking a series of
cases through the system from and back to the customer.
It was clear that the quality of the instructions from Head
Office were one cause of errors — they were ambiguous, in
different formats and amended by badly worded (not easy
to assimilate) updates. It would have been plausible at
that stage to believe that the problem had been identified
and without doubt a "control of procedures" approach
might have achieved some improvement with better instructions and better controlled documentation. However,
as the intrepid investigators proceeded, someone had a
different thought. There were, she observed, more fundamental problems.*

*The work procedures were split into technical and support
work — the technical work was performed by the professionals and the administrative work, for example typing,
was performed by office-based staff. Whilst observing
work going through branches she noted that the people
who did the technical work were handling cases entirely
unaided; they had their own personal case load. (And, as
it happens, they were measured on the number of cases
completed and ones outstanding.) Their work entailed being out on the road, remembering all the detailed requirements for many different customers and coping with
a large amount of "work in progress". This was, she observed, due to the historical structure of the organisation;
something which perhaps needed to be re-considered from
a "demand" or "flow" point of view. The way work was
currently being done had never been adjusted while new
and more complex demands were made on the system.
She came to the view that the fundamental structure was
the problem; no matter how good the instructions were,
the complexity being handled by the technical experts
would mean they were never going to produce accurate*

work. In simple terms, it is very difficult to get hundreds of people, spread all over the country, to handle a variety of tools in the same way — especially when the requirements keep changing. The current system included third-party inspection and double-checking, so the "procedures" route would only be likely to augment what was already a poor work system. It needed a radical re-think.

The team realised that their best strategy was to find a way to control all of the work as it came in from customers. They realised that they needed to put their very best resource on the front end to "clean up" and organise the customers' cases as they hit the system. The technical and administrative staff needed to be integrated and control of the work flow given to administrators. This would leave the technical people free to apply the skills that they were paid for. The measurement system had to change to measure flow rather than volume and revenue (they knew that if flow improved, service would improve and thus improvements in revenue and volume would follow).

It didn't stop there. They got engaged with one of their customers in looking at the whole process — beginning to end — from the customers' point of view and made changes to the way they worked together which improved the efficiency of both operations and improved service to the customer.

The question is, what is there in ISO 9000 which would have encouraged this organisation to think the way they needed to? Working to procedures would have been to treat the symptoms with no guarantee of not making the patient worse; the solution lay in understanding the organisation as a system, something not common amongst assessors.

Chapter 7

THE ISO 9000 ASSESSOR: AN AGENT FOR QUALITY?

The recent move by defenders of ISO 9000 to distinguish between registration and the Standard is no more than an acceptance that assessors have been influencing organisations to do things which are not in the organisations' best interests. To lay all the blame on the assessors is, perhaps, to miss the point. The assessors are just one of the influences. We have seen how assessors influence organisations to do things which are themselves causes of sub-optimisation. Beyond that, we have seen how it is in the assessors' interests to keep their clients registered. Assessors have achieved their status because of the marketplace coercion surrounding ISO 9000. Organisations, being obliged to register, have to seek help from somewhere and it would seem natural to seek it from those who are "supposed to know". The case studies in chapter 5 showed how assessors were often responsible for leading organisations to act in ways which sub-optimised performance.

To complete our case against ISO 9000 we have to look at who the assessors are, how they think about their role and understand more about why they encourage organisations to do the things they do.

The marketplace obligation surrounding ISO 9000 registration will inevitably lead to bad practice, and not only amongst assessors. We have met managers who are prepared to pay as much as £7,000 for a ready-made manual and "automatic" passes of assessments. The fact that this occurs is just one inevitable consequence of coercion. It is also probably true that managers indulging in such nefarious behaviour are seeking to avoid the grief associated with assessment — having to justify your actions to an outsider is not an attractive use of executive time, especially when one might reasonably doubt the assessor's expertise.

Anyone can become an ISO 9000 consultant, but only those who have been trained (and passed) can become an assessor. A brief look at what such training comprises ought to be enough to make one worry about the power invested in such a group. In summary, assessor training typically includes the following content:

- an overview of ISO 9000, its purpose and rationale
- interpreting each of the twenty clauses
- the role of the assessor
- guidelines for auditing
- "human" aspects: asking questions, dealing with conflict
- writing reports
- exercises and case studies.

No doubt there are assessors with extensive knowledge and experience (although we should always question the relevance of their experience to the needs of organisations today); but equally there will be people who know little, with only their newly gained qualification to guide them, finding themselves in positions of significant influence over the way organisations work.

Contrast these circumstances with those of Toyota, an organisation which has become a model of a "lean" system, producing extraordinary quality. The transformation was led by experts, people who worked with a hands-on approach. Their learning was developed through action (see Womack et al., 1991). The experts who led the transformation considered it normal to get "stuck in" in a practical way and to make the necessary changes. By contrast ISO 9000 positions quality through the means of a prescription — drawn up by our forebears — in the hands of (many) people who might have little or no hands-on experience. To make it worse, the auditor has power which, by and large, is exercised through observations of records and discussions in meeting rooms — talking about things, not doing things.

Auditing is not just a third-party activity. The Standard requires internal audits to be carried out as well. The training for auditors in one company was as follows:

- Step 1. Check the last audit report for the area you are auditing. Often they would have recommended areas for focus because of previously noticed problems (failures to follow procedures).

- Step 2. Select four or five areas to look at closely. The purpose of the audit is to check conformance to procedures and ensure that documents are being properly controlled.

- Step 3. Review the procedures employed for dealing with corrective actions and complaints in the area you are auditing.

The audit is designed to determine whether work is done according to the book. Nowhere does it focus on how well the process works — which ought to be the starting place. It is no surprise that audits of this kind give rise to objections from those who are audited. One correspondent put it this way:

> *"The basic internal audit system still suffers from lack of credibility. People who are being assessed will say: 'Yes, I know we're not doing that, but you don't understand the problems we have in this department. You're only the quality department'."*

It is perhaps an inevitable response when the quality department is independent of other functions and the people in quality perceive themselves as the experts. They have, after all, been bestowed with the power to take a view on how others are working. It was the thinking current in our organisations when we first embarked on this "quality management standards" journey — you have to have people's work checked by others. When the quality professionals discuss the problems of influencing others (as they see it), they argue that management support is required to overcome people's intransigence. It is to compound the same error. To argue that the quality department's credibility is greater when management support is stronger is to argue no more than "people will behave if they are coerced". It would be better to focus on why people behave as they do in the current system for, as we have seen, it is usually the system which influences their behaviour.

The image of many quality departments is one of judge, jury and executioner. While those in the quality department might argue that they are attempting to bring about compliance with ISO 9000 through influence rather than imposition, their means of "influence" are all coercive. Their role is to discover non-compliances and report them. A more user-friendly quality department might show the manager responsible what is required to prevent getting "caught" again, but even so it is hardly a way to win friends and influence people:

> *"The quality department gets asked who they are hunting when they walk around. People are heard to declare 'we shouldn't be saying this in front of the quality department'. People are even known to make the sign of the cross on seeing quality managers arrive on the scene."*

There are three important questions: Are the quality people auditing the right thing? Are they auditing it in the right way? Are their methods reliable? We have discussed the first at some length. The second is laid down by the Standard as a prescription. We should look briefly at the third before we continue.

ISO 9000 involves an audit process where auditors compare what they observe against a set of criteria. The quality question might be: Has this audit process been tested? We have never seen a group of auditors being sent independently to an organisation with the purpose of assessing the reliability of their audits. The only available evidence we have, from trainees on assessor courses, would suggest that if we were to research this phenomenon we would find inconsistencies between auditors.

> *"Even the trainers couldn't always agree what the correct interpretation was. I was stunned at the implications — we (the trainees) could find ourselves out in organisations, wielding tremendous power and, at the end of the day, telling people to do things which we felt were important. All this power after only three days training!"*

Another correspondent showed what the consequences of exercising this power were for him:

> *"I was trained as ISO lead assessor in 1991. We had a three-day course. The emphasis was placed entirely on compliance with the Standard. Our quality manager thought this was wonderful stuff. We raised deficiencies by the truckload. Few were fixed at all, and those that were signed off were just cosmetic fixes. I don't particularly relish confrontation and certainly don't want to be associated with 'losing' situations. I'm afraid auditing can have a lot of both."*

Assessors have told us that there are two distinct types of audit. One is a "compliance" audit, as practised by assessing organisations, which might be thought of as "pass/fail". The other is an "improvement" audit, which starts as a compliance audit and then moves on to explore what should be done to improve performance. There are many who argue that the assessing organisations should not offer consultancy or advice, as to stray outside "compliance" will result in less objectivity and the auditor's formal relationship would be at risk (not to say that commercial considerations could sway either advice or assessment results). These people often argue that only the internal audit function should be concerned with improvement. One correspondent felt the internal audit's most important function is to prevent ISO 9000 from stagnating. An interesting argument in that it ignores the need to find out why ISO 9000 *might* be stagnating.

As we have seen, the assessing organisations crossed the "compliance/advice" line some time ago, originally as a response to their clients who were complaining about the lack of value from the ISO 9000 audit and, more recently, in the offering (selling) of additional services which ostensibly claim to meet the client's developing needs.

The internal audit is considered as risky, weak or ineffective by many external assessors. Others often point out that an organisation could theoretically qualify (rather than formally register) for ISO 9000 if it has its own quality assurance system using in-house staff as auditors — thus any organisation could claim to be "ISO 9000 compliant". However, many external assessors assert that the standard of internal quality auditing leaves a lot to be desired:

> *"It's frequently questionable as to whether internal audit is really effective in identifying non-conformances to the Standard and acting as an initiator of corrective action. The required internal quality audits should also be undertaken to the recognised standard (ISO 10011-1). In practice, this is rarely the case, with people with little or no training and little understanding of quality or of the requirements of the Standard carrying out internal audits."*

The importance of using properly trained assessors provides a marketing opportunity for assessing organisations:

"A frequent non-conformance I see raised against smaller companies is that of not having any staff trained in quality systems auditing."

In smaller organisations, we often find that internal audits are carried out by managers in order to prevent the additional costs of auditing staff:

"I once met the managing director of a manufacturing company employing about thirty people who told me that once a year he 'had a walk round and made sure everyone was doing their jobs properly'. When I asked what was the view of his certification body to this approach he grinned and told me that they had held their certificate for four years and had never been threatened with having it revoked! By having to submit to third party surveillance visits at least it meant that their quality system was audited correctly occasionally — although what actual benefit this brought to potential customers of this firm was also questionable."

The assessors, however, are suspicious of organisations which rely on their own auditing:

"When I conduct a second-party audit, if I find internal auditors giving their company a clean bill of health I get very suspicious. Are they looking hard enough? Almost inevitably not."

Another was concerned with the frequency of external assessments:

"A weak link is the frequency of surveillance visits. Most small companies get a visit once a year, and so their ISO certificate carries little more weight than my motor's MOT certificate."

The assessors are preoccupied with a view of quality as inspection and control, a view whose roots are in traditional "command and control" management thinking. Our experience has taught us to take a different view, because of the perspective which we have learned and from which we understand organisations. To take a simple example: if an audit shows that people are not working to procedures, one view might be that to change the way procedures are written or to spend more time explaining the whys and wherefores will solve the problem. This view assumes that people "should" work to procedures and that the procedures are right. A better view would be to question first of all why people find it necessary to avoid their procedures. This is not the same as saying that people should not work to procedures (as is often heard by the defenders). It is to start with a view about what it is that is affecting performance and it could lead to completely different conclusions about what should be done. The "quality priority" is learning, not controlling people's behaviour.

The power of their position has an impact on the assessors' behaviour — something which people can't resist describing to others, as it has caused so much irritation to themselves. Here is one example:

> *"I've got one of those little anecdotes for you. . . . I can't remember whether this was the first visit, the actual inspection to see if we comply, or on a follow-up audit, but . . . I collected the external auditors from reception to take them for a coffee and ask them where they wanted to go. (Thinks . . . must have been an early visit — there were two of them. . . .) As he shook hands the 'leader' said, 'I'll just point out a minor non-conformance for you . . . the Quality Policy you have hanging here in reception is not dated.'*
>
> *We had to reprint all the policy signs we had in every office with a date on the bottom and get the MD to sign them all again. As a result our quality improved rapidly*

(not), and our customers were even more pleased than before (not).

Ever since then my respect for external auditors and assessors has always been tempered by a wee bit of suspicion about the potential 'jobs-worths' out there who could ruin a company's reputation by withdrawing certification, not for something so trivial, but for something which may be a matter of judgement."

An ISO 9000 assessor responded to this story as follows:

"There are two possible responses in this situation. The more polite one is to ask the 'assessor' to explain the non-conformance — by reference to the appropriate clause of the Standard. I have had similar comments from assessors (and I am one myself) — and have always found the above approach to be best. What you are really saying is 'prove to me that you are stating fact, rather than personal opinion'. Even if he could provide some kind of supporting evidence for this — he still scores 0/10 for tact — this is not a good way to start an assessment! Trouble is — people still treat assessment organisations with some kind of reverence — when all's said and done they're only another supplier, after all."

But they are not. Assessment organisations are the arbiters of (perceived) market acceptability with all the power that accrues to such a position. It is a power which is easily abused. Cognisant of this abuse of power, one consultant saw this as his remedy:

"Whenever possible, I try to attend assessments and surveillance visits with my clients — this cuts down on the 'Chinese whispers' — and sometimes cause the 'eager assessor' to think twice before leaping on his/her particular 'hobby horse'. In these situations always introduce your-

*self with a business card that says 'Lead Assessor' —
makes the point !!"*

And now we have the policeman for the policeman. A folly beyond all follies. And we are supposed to be improving our organisations? Can we or should we attempt to improve the
quality of our organisations through audit? The argument for
auditing is that only an external agency should conduct an
evaluation to establish that we are a quality company. Leaving
aside all the problems with how assessors interpret the Standard and what they look for, the whole idea of independent
evaluation takes us away from where the focus ought to be, i.e.
that *we* know how we are doing, that *we* can build in methods
for improvement and *we* can work with our suppliers/
customers to continually improve performance. Assessment via
a third party is, of itself, a potential barrier to learning and
improvement.

This is not a view shared by the assessing community. They
feel that formalising (documenting) the way an organisation
works is central to improving performance. Here is one assessor's view of a what he called a "well-thought-out quality
strategy":

*"The most successful organisations begin with a sound
strategic planning process that includes improvement objectives and policy deployment techniques."*

Sounds quite sensible, but if managers were to set off on strategic planning and goal-setting they might actually end up in
trouble. We would ask how an organisation can sensibly set
objectives for improvement without first understanding its
current capability? Kenichi Ohmae had this to say about strategy (interspersed with the language we have used in this
book):

*"Of course it is important to take the competition into ac-
count, but that should not come first in making strategy.*

> *First comes painstaking analysis of the needs of custom-*
> *ers* [what matters to customers?]. *First comes close*
> *analysis of a company's real degrees of freedom in re-*
> *sponding to those needs* [what is our capability?]. *First*
> *comes the willingness to re-think, fundamentally, what*
> *products* [and services] *are and what they do as well as*
> *how best to organise the business system that designs,*
> *builds and markets them* [how does our system work to
> deliver that capability?]" *(Ohmae, 1990).*

What Ohmae is saying is that strategy begins by looking inside an organisation, knowing how and how well the organisation responds to the needs of customers. The assessor's ideas could, by contrast, be easily translated by managers into choosing "objectives" in the way that managers "traditionally" choose targets, without any understanding of how and whether they will be achieved — what Deming referred to as "goals without methods". As for "policy deployment techniques", there is no doubt that in a "value stream"-oriented culture, it could be a powerful and systematic way of deploying improvement. In a "command and control" culture, however, it could easily mean a kind of "turbo ISO 9000".

To return to the assessor's argument:

> *"Another part of the foundation is a documented quality*
> *system for controlling routine aspects of work and proc-*
> *esses."*

Again this sounds sensible. But wouldn't an understanding of current performance be better? To place value on a documented quality system one should first be assured that what is documented is what happens. And, furthermore, is documentation the best way to control work? But to continue with his argument:

> *"Building upon that, these 'World Class' organisations*
> *implement a continuous improvement process tailored to*

*suit their culture. This provides the opportunity for people
throughout the organisation to become involved in identi-
fying improvement opportunities and contributing their
creative solutions."*

Again this sounds sensible — people are, after all, the most
important asset and it would be beneficial to have everyone
involved. Quite how continuous improvement processes suit
cultures he doesn't say, but we can think of one distinction:
Command-and-control managers typically see continuous improvement as people doing projects on their work processes,
perhaps with management direction and reviews. Joining a
"corrective-action team" or the like is "an opportunity to be involved". How many such initiatives run into the sand because
the teams find themselves up against the prevailing culture —
that is, the way the organisation currently works? Effective
change requires action on the system; that always requires
more than generating ideas and willingness to contribute.

The assessor's next assertion is the one which worried us
the most:

*"As the fourth element, the most successful organisations
will have reward and recognition systems which reinforce
the types of change that are required for long-term success. Few managers realise that all of their 'quality' efforts are about change — changing people's habits, attitudes, and behaviours (including management) toward
new processes and paradigms. If the reward and recognition system isn't aligned with their goals, managers and
their people will have a strong tendency to slip back into
their old ways."*

Now we doubt how much he really knows about quality. When
organisations use reward and recognition systems to reinforce
the desired outcomes, sub-optimisation always occurs. This is
not to say that reward and recognition systems are not impor-

tant, it is usually vitally important to remove them if they are contingent in nature (contingent meaning "do this, to get that") as contingent rewards always worsen performance. The strong tendency he observes for people to "slip back into their old ways" is usually a further reflection on the design of the system. It is management's job to change the system. But back to our assessor:

"So, for what it's worth, that is my general approach to 'TQM'. An ISO 9000 quality system can be a valuable component, or some other model may be appropriate. But, the bottom line is that all of these elements are needed. Too many managers and practitioners become enamoured with empowerment and tools and techniques without any real clue as to where they're going . . ."

But does *he* know where *he* is going? What looked like quite sensible advice had potential flaws when considered in more detail. When managers are presented with similar advice it is not surprising that they should be attracted to the rational, "common-sense" ideas; they are ideas which might fit with their current ("command and control") view of the world — that goals should be set and cascaded, that people should be controlled through procedures, that incentives will drive the behaviour you want and that everybody should be involved in teams. As we have observed before, it might be wiser to find out why people do not currently feel involved — what is it about the current system that makes people behave the way they do?

When things go wrong, the assessors are, quite naturally, inclined to blame the managers:

"As with any enterprise opportunity (sic) *there are managers who care only for the bottom line and not ethics. They bring the business into disrepute and those they af-*

fect will naturally become cynical. There are more of them
about than is realised."

At this point we tend to get confused. We learned from Deming
that quality is a better way to run a business. Quality results
in greater productivity, more revenue, cheaper processes and
so on. If our correspondent is saying that many managers care
only for output or budgetary data and use the same in ways
which in fact sub-optimise performance we would agree with
him. However, he wants to distinguish ethics as representative
of quality. Which leads us back to an argument we have already heard — what matters is how you interpret the Standard:

> *"The Standards published today are not generic. They*
> *were initially intended for the control of military suppli-*
> *ers and have evolved over the years to embrace a wider*
> *manufacturing base but are, as yet, nowhere near wide*
> *enough in scope to be truly appropriate to all business sec-*
> *tors. This poses problems during implementation and can*
> *lead to interpretation issues which in turn can lead to fur-*
> *ther dispute and criticism. The Standards and compli-*
> *ance to them are in no way essential and should not be*
> *regarded, and in fact cannot be regarded, as the de facto*
> *mechanism to ensure quality output and consultants*
> *should not preach otherwise."*

However, consultants thrive on the "OK if you do it right" argument. The problem with "OK if you do it right" is that it
fails to account for what has happened. To accept this argument is to accept that we should continue to extend this Standard in the face of abundant stupidity. But the consultants lay
the blame at the manager's door. For example, one said:

> *"Most companies seek ISO 9000 for the wrong reasons*
> *and do not gain improvements from implementing it.*
> *Most truly don't understand ISO, Quality, and systems."*

We asked whether he would not agree that the most parsimonious explanation of the damage caused by ISO 9000 registration was that the managers and their advisors were preoccupied with notions of control rather than improvement. He replied:

"Yes, I agree that a good portion are preoccupied with control, but with many I wouldn't even give them credit for that."

The damage evident in the case studies was in part due to the assessors' (and managers') interpretation of the Standard, in part due to the requirements of the Standard itself but also due to the way these companies (and others) go about ISO 9000 registration. The usual prescription that an organisation is encouraged to follow in order to register to ISO 9000 is as follows:

1. **Look at your current organisation to see how it compares with the requirements of the Standard**. What would such a view reveal? Perhaps lack of a formal contract review, procedures not documented, differences in working practices, "sloppy" methods, "reinventing wheels", lack of formal procedures for people to work to and so on. Would changing these things lead to improvements in performance? Sometimes yes, sometimes no. This starting place reflects the plausible aspiration to "do things right". The focus of registration to ISO 9000 becomes "what do we need to do to achieve registration?", regardless of whether these are the "right things" to do. Taking a look at the current organisation is "conditioned" by the wording of the Standard. Is this the best way to "take a look"? We do not believe so.

2. **What corrective action is needed to conform to the Standard?** Whether or not these actions will improve performance is not asked. Such a view is made all the more difficult because the analysis did not start with per-

formance, as it should. It started with comparison to the Standard. The corrective actions typically generated are concerned with the establishment and control of documented procedures. Not only is it questionable whether these procedures will improve performance, but the more pressing query is whether the effort in establishing and maintaining them adds to the economic vitality of the organisation, or is it essentially a drain on both resources and morale.

3. **Prepare a programme of work**. It becomes important to establish by when all corrective actions can expect to be achieved. The focus of the work becomes achievement of the plan, rather than improving performance.

4. **Define, document and implement new procedures**. Procedures are always central to the plan. They are the means by which assessors can do *their* work.

5. **Prepare a quality manual**. This ties together all of the procedures. It shows all procedures by which the organisation should be managed.

6. **Pre-assessment meeting**. The chosen assessor usually recommends a pre-assessment meeting to help the client establish their suitability for going forward to assessment. The interpretation of ISO 9000's requirements for the particular circumstances is the focus for discussion. As we have observed, this discussion is coloured by the assessor's interpretation of the Standard.

7. **Assessment**. The assessor determines whether the organisation conforms to its documentation.

8. **Registration**.

ISO 9000 is supposed to be used to make sure that a given supplier has the capability of meeting a technical standard and delivering a good quality product or service. Now we know how it is typically implemented, it is easy to see how it is open to the charge that it does not guarantee that a supplier really delivers a product adequate for a precise purpose. The Standard is designed for assessing a company's quality system or "management system", but the means by which that system is established are likely to ensure that at best the system is controlling the status quo, and at worst performance will deteriorate. Perhaps they should be called eight steps to suboptimisation.

Change by this method is highly likely to do nothing for performance, or make it worse. The place from which to start change is an understanding of your current organisation.

Rather than focus on how the organisation compares to a Standard, management should take a long hard look at the organisation's core processes, those which touch the customer. Work is either:

- Value creating — defined by being in the core process. If ISO 9000 has been of any value it is here in terms of a spur to creating order and clarity.

- Non-value creating from the point of view of the customer, but necessary for running the business at the moment (much of the work associated with ISO 9000 is of this type; for example, registration enables organisations to tender but adds no value for the customer in operational terms).

- Non-value creating and unnecessary or even counterproductive. This type of activity can be "cut out" with impunity. As we have seen, ISO 9000 creates a lot of this.

In our experience, it is vital that the leader "sees" the problems first-hand. This means "rolling up sleeves" and getting out into the work processes. It means commissioning work teams to map and diagnose current work processes and then listening carefully to what they have found and leading action (some actions the work team can take, others go across organisational boundaries and thus require leadership to make progress).

Leaders need to learn about how the organisation creates value (or does not, as the case may be) at the level of the work processes; they need to learn about how to change work at this level. In the course of their work leaders also discover how the "old" methods of change cause interference rather than improvement. If leaders do not anchor their understanding in the performance of their current processes, it increases the probability that they will slip back to "managing by the numbers" and other practices of "command and control". Leaders who do develop good knowledge about their work processes learn to take an alternative "common sense" view of the work, a view based on regarding the organisation as a system. Once a picture of their organisation "as a system" has been created, managers can go through the organisation, one process at a time, to discover how their current methods and thinking contribute to purpose and to what extent they currently cause sub-optimisation. It is fundamental to taking a different view that the current assumptions and practices are brought to the surface and shown, in practical terms and in relation to performance.

A software support organisation was registered to ISO 9000. The means by which they handled customers' calls was documented and any assessor, internal or external, could visit and be satisfied that they "did as they said they did". They were proud to proclaim that they "treated all customers the same". When they looked at what mattered to customers (what each customer's nominal value was) they soon realised that it was foolish to treat all calls and all customers as the same. To do so was creating costs. By looking at their organisation as a system, the managers learned that, for example, their customers were often subject to responses which were entirely out of synch with their needs; their current measures (of activity) were causing waste. For the first time they could "see" what needed to be done. The cry for change brought the ISO 9000 managers out from their lair. "You can't change anything without going through the correct procedures for change," they pro-

claimed. Their advice was ignored. It was more important to experiment with and learn from designing different responses to different nominal values than be subjected to the draining influence of justifying everything first.

Auditors get uncomfortable when you remove the means for them to do their work. But in so many cases we have found that the justification for action is "because it is a requirement of the auditor" rather than a requirement of the customer. This was a system which changed from taking an attitude of "you are in our procedures" to taking an attitude of "we'll design our response around your particular need". Simple, radical, but difficult to achieve if the organisation is being governed by "procedures first" thinking, by people who demand that activity satisfies the requirements for auditing above learning about how well something satisfies the requirements of the customer.

We worry about the quality of the assessors. People in organisations worry about the quality of assessors. The assessors worry about the quality of assessors. Be that as it may, the assessor has achieved a position of power and, inevitably, we are finding evidence that this power is being abused.

One Organisation's Experience

"Lease Co." is a leasing company. They were amongst the first in their sector to register to ISO 9000. We got talking about their experiences with ISO 9000 when the quality manager told us that he was getting concerned about his assessor. But before looking at his concerns, let's look at the context:

Lease Co. had recently re-structured its operations into customer-facing business teams. The teams ran their operations as complete businesses. It was a striking contrast to their old "functional" organisation. The quality manager was appointed to his role as part of the re-structuring. He had been involved in the introduction of ISO 9000 (then BS 5750) as a line manager; this was his recollection of that time:

"Looking back, we were being led by people who were acknowledged by others as exponents of best practice, hence there was no questioning of their expertise. We felt that registration would give us kudos and, more importantly, we needed it to tender for contracts with Government and large organisations in the private sector. I remember feeling it was rather like the civil service, having everything documented. The message was procedures. We didn't think in those days about processes, as we do now, and you could say that ISO 9000 was a start in that direction. But in truth it was concerned with procedures.

There was a lot of excitement as we prepared for the first assessment. Everything concentrated on what I would call the policing elements of our business. People were implored to read their procedures, they were asked if they knew how to do things in accordance with the procedures ('how do you handle a complaint, how do you issue a controlled document'); we even had notices in the loo reminding people to read their procedures!

With hindsight, it would have been better if we had controlled it, rather than it controlling us. It became the be-all and end-all. Managers were chastised if their procedures were not up-to-date and everyone was expected to handle work in a manner consistent with the procedures."

This was (and still is) the story for many organisations. The real driver was "getting and keeping the Standard". What had been documented was controlling people's behaviour. It was vital to keep to the documentation because otherwise the worst could happen — they could fail an assessment. This was the real fear, it was fear of the assessor.

New to the job, the quality manager had a difficult task ahead of him. He had been appointed in August and an assessment was due in October. The organisation had been restructured and so the written procedures needed a complete review; on top of that the new teams were starting to work their own (preferred) ways — after all, theirs were the businesses to run.

To the delight of the business teams, he took the decision that he and his assistant would worry about the procedures. He recognised that he had little time and he rightly saw his role as a support to the businesses. It was probably the only way the organisation could be assured to be ready for the assessor's visit in October. Three months' hard work ensued, taking out procedures which were examples of "over-egging the pudding", establishing what were the core work processes for all business teams, establishing and agreeing new procedures and so on. They made it. It was only during the assessor's visit that the quality manager started to have doubts — doubts about the assessment as a contribution to his business and doubt about the assessor:

"Not having had an assessment before I asked how I should behave and was told that my predecessor had taken the assessor on a tour of the facilities. I gave up a week of my time and 'chaperoned' him around the UK. The auditor had power and he behaved as though he knew it. He would ask to see something and it would be brought. He would ask to meet someone and their schedule would be changed to accommodate him. That would have been tolerable if I had felt as though we were being properly audited, but it didn't feel like that to me.

The assessor would constantly assert that ISO 9000 was a management system, as though we should appreciate the gravity of his assertion, yet he would focus on nit-picking details, for example whether pages were numbered in a document. We had striven hard to create a documented system which reflected the way the new structure worked and what we were expecting was a rigorous audit of what we had done. We wanted to know how well we had done it and we wanted to know how we could improve. We got

*neither. We didn't feel as though we had been assessed.
The only non-conformances noted were ones we had
pointed out."*

Following the disappointment of the assessment experience
(which they passed), the quality manager had further cause for
concern. His assessor had recommended a course of training
for a group of staff. Another consultant from the assessor's organisation made a proposal. As it happened, the consultant
proposing the training came from another part of the country
and the quality manager discovered that the original assessor
was monitoring the success or failure of this proposal because
it counted on his "numbers". The assessing organisation had
given their regional managers revenue targets. With what
damage to performance? Who knows, but now we know how
much the assessor's organisation understood quality.

> *"The process felt like 'you scratch my back and I'll scratch
> yours'. I was contributing to him meeting his budget. Now
> when I look back I am suspicious. The assessor persuaded
> us to treat our three businesses separately for the purposes
> of registration when we used to treat two as the off-shoots
> of the first, and assess them all together. Now I'm con-
> cerned that this simply represents a way to get more reve-
> nue from us. If we don't continue to go for registration,
> where will his revenue come from?"*

It is now more than ten years since their original registration.
It is only now that the business is organised into processes
which reflect the life-cycle of its customers. It is only now that
they are starting to measure performance in a way which leads
to improvement. They could have been ten years further down
the path.

Chapter 8

CONCLUSION: THE CASE AGAINST ISO 9000

"It makes a lot of sense if you don't think about it"
Dagwood Bumstead

Hindsight is a wonderful thing. It is easy to see how we would have been far better-off if, in 1979, we had embarked on a programme of education for all managers to help them understand and manage their organisations as systems. It was the fundamental assumption behind Deming's teachings in Japan, and an assumption which remains against the grain of what we have described as traditional, "command and control" management thinking. Instead, we have adopted and promulgated a quality management standard which has led us away from understanding quality and sub-optimised the performance of our organisations.

Despite the accumulation of evidence which ought to make us all profoundly antagonistic to ISO 9000, the bandwagon rolls on. Today the power lies with the little-known committees whose job it is to amend ISO 9000's clauses for its continued promulgation. The committees will not call a halt — they work on the assumption it is here to stay — nor will the plethora of others who have emotional or financial investments in ISO 9000's continuation. If a halt is to be called it is the managers in organisations who will have to be the ones to act. It is in their interests to do so. They are the ones who face the serious consequences of this misguided phenomenon; they are the ones who stand to gain when they are no longer subjected to the strictures of the Standard; they are the ones who will become empowered through learning that there is a better way.

Before we offer a little advice to the manager who "knows" that ISO 9000 is the wrong thing to do, let us review the arguments against ISO 9000 set out in chapter 1.

1.   ISO 9000 encourages organisations to act in ways which make things worse for their customers.

The intention was that ISO 9000 registration would give organisations (note: not ordinary consumers) confidence in suppliers. Yet everyone can point to suppliers who ship late, ship the wrong goods, make mistakes with invoicing, are difficult to do business with, upset their customers and yet are still registered to ISO 9000. We have given examples of the same throughout this book; they are neither unusual nor, unfortunately, to be unexpected.

It is the clause known as "contract review" which is the cause of some of these problems. We have already observed that the contractual, defensive thinking associated with contract review might have been an appropriate short-term response to the problems of munitions supply during the War; it might have been one way to hold the suppliers of power stations and the like to their contract, but this is not quality thinking. Moreover, this clause has been applied with dreadful consequences in many service organisations, which stress that: "You are to get service this way because these are our procedures." When customers experience poor service they vote with their feet. ISO 9000 is responsible for a lot of poor service experiences; registration increases the probability that an organisation will be worse from it's customers' point of view.

2.   Quality by inspection is not quality.

"Document what you do" and "prove that you do it" is the ISO 9000 view of the world. Proof means inspection, inspection requires evidence and evidence means documentation. Where would we be if we had no requirement to produce documentation for everything we do? What would performance be like if our focus was learning rather than proof?

Recently we worked with a professional services organisation. Before they changed the way they worked they had procedures for everything — how the customers' demands should be logged and acted on, all the way through the various steps to resolution. All demands were subjected to the same procedures. The organisation had been registered to ISO 9000 for five years and its performance was described as stable and relatively poor (moderate customer satisfaction and productivity when compared to others). They took a view of their organisation as a system. It became evident that what mattered to customers was not what was being delivered by the system; customers had differing demands, thus it made no sense to treat them to the same procedures. They decided to run the organisation as a system. Every customer demand should create its own procedure; the professional advisers should continually monitor the nature of demand to know what was predictable and what was unpredictable. No longer should they "work to procedures". Instead, control should be effected through continuous monitoring of demand, throughput and customer satisfaction. They doubled their throughput, halved the average time it took to solve customer problems and improved customer satisfaction for the first time in 15 years. As a corollary, morale improved. Control moved to where it was needed to enable high performance and learning.

ISO 9000 registration had been one of the barriers to this happening. Inspecting work as adherence to procedures had been controlling the wrong things.

3. ISO 9000 starts from the flawed presumption that work is best controlled by specifying and controlling procedures.

People often say that procedures must be a "good thing". This is the way one correspondent put it:

> *"We all work to procedures in some way, form or other in our daily lives. Voluntarily and involuntarily. Our own individual lifestyle in the modern world is built around procedures. Some written in law and others by habit or etiquette. Without the visible and invisible rules we would surely drop into chaos. This analogy can be equally applied to the work-place in any environment. The company takes the view that it wishes to make money. In order to do that it must make or do something that attracts customers. To maintain customers and to broaden its sales area it must go on satisfying customers. To ensure that this philosophy is understood by all a policy is established which is supported by a set of rules that govern output. The management maintain control over its production or service. Discipline is maintained and output stabilised."*

So procedures provide us with order and predictability. But he has not addressed how. What does this "philosophy" mean? How is management thinking translated into action? What does "discipline" mean? Adherence to documented procedures or bringing your brain to work? Adherence to procedures will control output, but is that what we want? Does lack of procedures lead to chaos? The professional services organisation maintained greater clarity about its purpose and achieved greater control by removing procedures and managing the organisation as a system. The difference is the starting place. Starting with data concerning achievement versus purpose (How well do we deliver what matters to customers? What is our capability in terms of throughput?) is a prerequisite for learning and improvement; starting with documentation and control of procedures implicitly assumes that we know about the nature of demand and we also know the best way to handle it. Any variation in demand not accounted for by the procedures will lead to problems. In other words, establishing procedures can result in greater chaos (increased variation).

Another correspondent attributed the problem to who writes the procedures:

> *"The problem often with people writing quality procedures is that the sort of folk who want to write them are the last sort of folk who should be allowed to. And it all turns into yet another example of management (the activity) quietly turning into an end in its own right — people thinking they've created something new when they 'capture' things in diagrams or procedures, people thinking their quality is better because they have written it down, and people thinking that their people will perform better because we've handcuffed them to a bureaucratic inefficiency we call a procedure."*

It is "management activity turning into an end in its own right" that causes so many problems — the concern to "get everyone working to procedures by a certain date" and "policing" deviation. The assumption is that people should work to procedures, but it is not always apparent that this is the right thing to do. The correspondent goes on to say:

> *"If using the procedure is easier than not using it, people will do it. That is far more likely to be the case if there is some automation assisting the correct route."*

But if automation controls the route — and this is the rationale of many software packages — the results can be disastrous: workflow controlled by computers not people, leaving people feeling controlled, not "in control". People have to feel in control if they are to improve their work processes. Control through procedures encourages attention to people's behaviour

(Did they do as they should?) rather than encouraging attention to the process and its purpose (How well is this working?).

> *The claims administrators in an insurance office had to*
> *enter the class of risk in the electronic claim form. The*
> *form would not move on if fields were uncompleted. With*
> *the usual sense of demoralisation caused by work stan-*
> *dards and 'people management', it became common prac-*
> *tice to 'give the machine anything that will mean it moves*
> *along'.*

The problem is not with control per se, but with the nature of
control. ISO 9000 encourages control of people's behaviour
through inspection of their adherence to procedures. Control is
effected through internal and external audits. The purpose of
documentation is to establish "what we say we do" and to allow
the audit process to determine "whether we do it". It is no
more than a method of controlling output. To control work in
this way is to take the view that quality is about conformance
and consistency. It is not. Quality is about improvement.

Quality teaches different thinking about control. If you
want genuine control (which will help improve performance),
you need measures which are related to purpose and the
measures need to be in the hands of people doing the work —
something many ISO 9000 assessors would not condone.

4. The typical method of implementation is bound to cause sub-optimisation of performance.

Remember that the recommended method for implementing
ISO 9000 is to read the Standard; understand its requirements; look at your business to audit the position today; identify gaps between today's position and the requirements of the
Standard; develop a plan to close the gap; and, finally, implement the plan. The focus of implementation becomes achievement of the plan — it may or may not relate to improved performance. So often we have found organisations focusing on

what they need to do to achieve or maintain registration, regardless of whether this activity is improving or hindering business performance.

This recommended method is bound to cause sub-optimisation of performance because, quite simply, it takes no account of what is governing current performance. Without such knowledge, managers make changes to their organisations at their peril. It is no surprise that ISO 9000 has become viewed as "extra work" in many organisations — it is. Additional activities are developed because of the requirements of the Standard or its agent (the assessor), not for the benefits they bring to performing and improving work.

On the other hand, to know what is predictable about current performance and what governs it is a strong position from which to manage change. However, we have never met an ISO 9000 assessor or consultant who understands and knows how to act on this simple principle.

5. The Standard relies too much on people's, and particularly assessors', interpretation of quality.

The assessors subscribe to the "control through procedures" philosophy. The documented procedures provide the means for the assessor to do their work. It is in their interest, then, to ensure that procedures they would like to see are the ones they do see. We have seen how the assessor influences the decisions made around implementation and documentation, but it is not just the assessor who brings interpretation to bear. The Standard says little about how specifics should be implemented, leaving plenty of space for interpretation by all who have some involvement.

Should we solve the problem of interpretation by generating more specific advice and guidance? The architects of QS 9000 would appear to think so. We have found such "rational" methods to be amongst the least effective in achieving change. Effective change starts with an understanding of the whats and hows of current performance: What do we know about the performance of this process? What are the current measures in use and what can we learn from them? Can current measures tell us about the performance of a process in relation to its purpose? Are the current measures causing sub-optimisation? What measures do we need to get to learn more about what is going on? Would these new measures be useful for those who work in this process to enable them to effect better control and, hence, improvement? These questions would open the issues which matter to quality and performance improvement. They are not, in our experience, found in the repertoire of the ISO 9000 assessor.

One final example of the typical ISO 9000 assessor's thinking: During a visit with a client who had reached the short-list for the UK Business Excellence award, we learned that one of the assessing team was also an ISO 9000 assessor. Apparently he had asked a supervisor why she didn't count the mail coming into and out of her section, for activity records and traceability. "We'd rather just deal with it," was her reply. God bless her, and keep us from these people who would have us build waste into our organisations.

6. The Standard promotes, encourages, and explicitly demands actions which cause sub-optimisation.

Documentation and its associated work is the most obvious, contract review masquerading as customer service is another. Add to those the principles of inspection (internal and external) and independent control of people's work and you have what is, in effect, a recipe for sub-optimisation. But the causes of sub-optimisation go beyond the physical. The ethos of ISO 9000 is a major cause of demoralisation amongst people who have to do the work, in itself more damaging than all of the above. Pride is the most important source of motivation. For pride to be engaged, people need to be in control. That requires a different philosophy and practice; it requires a different system.

7. When people are subjected to external controls, they will be inclined to pay attention to only those things which are affected by the controls.

So they do what they have to, to pass the audit. The market-place coercion surrounding ISO 9000 is the primary cause of a failure to learn. "Do what it takes" won't open management's eyes to what is going on in their organisations and once the goal is achieved little attention is paid to what might be important. It is for this reason that most managers know little about ISO 9000; it has not been felt either necessary or important to learn about it and/or question it. Coercion or obligation has resulted in lack of attention; lack of attention has blinded managers to what is arguably the most important subject on the management curriculum.

8. ISO 9000 has discouraged managers from learning about the theory of variation.

The "inspection" school has maintained the upper hand. The "variation" school is different and profoundly more valuable as a means to performance improvement. The inspection school plays to the familiar; it encompasses recognisable notions. The variation school is unfamiliar and not immediately logical if you have a traditional, "command and control" view of the world.

Managers do not need to know how to construct a control chart, but they need to know how to think and apply the principles of variation to their system. They need to know how to act rather than react. They need to think of their role in terms of prediction rather than control. They need to appreciate the distinction between costs and their causes and to use the theory of variation to help them find and remove the latter. And costs should not be construed as relating to functions or activity, they should relate to whole processes delivering service to customers. Processes go across organisational boundaries as well as across functional boundaries.

9.   ISO 9000 has failed to foster good customer–supplier relations.

In every sector we have seen obligations being placed on suppliers to become registered to ISO 9000; "You comply or we won't buy" being the grossest manifestation. Instead of coercing suppliers to register to ISO 9000, organisations could have been working with their suppliers to improve their common lot. That is the way it has been in the Toyota organisation for the last forty years; the results are striking. In every sector we have studied we hear words like "partnership" and "co-operation" but we see deeds which differ. Coercion to register to ISO 9000 is just one manifestation of the contractual, hands-off way traditional managers conduct customer–supplier relations, but it is probably the most visible manifestation of what is a contractual rather than co-operative attitude.

10.   As an intervention, ISO 9000 has not encouraged managers to think differently.

ISO 9000 is a particular manifestation of traditional "command and control" management thinking. "Command" people to work to procedures, "control" them through inspection. ISO 9000 maintains a management tradition which itself needs to change if we are to compete on the world stage. It is not a "first step" on the road to becoming a quality organisation, as is so often argued; it is keeping step with a tradition which needs to be broken. With those who argue that it is a first step, we argue the following: If UK plc were a "quality organisation" and its "product" was the quality Standard, on the basis of what we know about the impact of this Standard on performance would we not "stop production" now? ISO 9000 is not "fit for purpose". It is, on the contrary, getting in the way.

Epilogue

SO WHAT CAN WE DO
ABOUT ISO 9000?

How can we "stop production"? Our whole system is driving
the growth of ISO 9000: Government supports it; Training and
Enterprise Councils (TECs) are targeted on promulgating it;
public sector and some of the larger private sector organisations insist their suppliers register to it; some motor manufacturers are (in our opinion) foolish enough to add more detail to
the requirements and make it mandatory for their suppliers.
Where would you intervene on a system like this? How can we
provide the sharpest halt to this phenomenon?

You might think that Government is the place to start. We
drew a blank. Their response is guided by their advice; advice
is provided by those who have created the ISO 9000 industry.
The TECs cannot be encouraged to fight it; they are measured
on their ability to promote ISO 9000 (we have even been prevented from talking to some TEC audiences about ISO 9000 as
our views are not consistent with their "policy"). We doubt that
change will be achieved through the institutions, and if change
does occur by this route it will be slow. We cannot afford to
take time. Rapid change will only occur if there is strong pressure from the market, if managers raise their voices, cease
registration and take whatever action they feel is necessary.
Democracy does work. Whenever we discuss our findings with
large groups of managers we find they agree with what we
have to say; the few who argue in its defence constitute a tiny
minority. If every manager who has doubts expressed the same

to their Member of Parliament, Trade Association, Training and Enterprise Council, fellow managers, customers and suppliers, we believe ISO 9000 would wither quickly.

We take heart that many of those responsible for the "marketplace coercion" in larger organisations are beginning to lessen their adherence to ISO 9000 as a mandatory requirement of suppliers:

> *"Someone I know, who works in the QA department of a major electronics supplier to the MoD, has told me that they tend to have more quality problems with their ISO registered suppliers than with those who don't have it. He also said that they have recently had their budget increased for undertaking second-party audits of their suppliers. In this case, where is the value in requiring ISO certification?"*

In mid-1996 we learned that the Australian Federal Government had relaxed its requirement that suppliers should be registered to ISO 9000. The Minister for small businesses had listened to the complaints of those who felt that ISO 9000 was damaging economic performance — complaints which were the same as were heard in the UK. It suggests that the Australians were more prepared to act when needs be, rather than defend the status quo.

In late 1996 we received the following e-mail:

> *"Last night, I was privileged to attend a meeting with regard to ISO 9000 standards concerning the safety of flight hardware and flight systems. The FAA (Federal Aviation Administration, USA) has dealt a blow that may affect us as aircraft manufacturers, in the manner in which we shall perform our tasks under this misguided "quality" banner. The FAA has apparently rejected the notion of recognising ISO!!! There is no doubt in my mind that we*

> *are waking up to the misgivings and futile promises that this system claims to promote."*

So the first advice we have for anyone who is concerned about what to do about ISO 9000 is: *Do not assume that it is here to stay.*

The signals from the UK Government are weak at the moment. The UK is the "home" of ISO 9000; with all the effort that has gone into persuading other countries to adopt it, it is perhaps unsurprising that the UK does not take the lead in questioning its efficacy. However, UK trade associations are beginning to respond to demands from their members for an improvement to the situation and, in turn, this pressure is having a limited impact on the Department of Trade and Industry (DTI). One correspondent observed this shift:

> *"Even the DTI have changed their views recently — they now agree that for some smaller businesses ISO 9000 is not necessarily appropriate. A somewhat different line from that put out during the days of the 'money-go-round'."*

But it has to be said this is not much of a shift and, as we have observed, to argue that it is "more costly for smaller firms" is to miss the point. It is to accept that ISO 9000 represents a cost; probably the best "quality joke" of the century.

Remember that there is no evidence to suggest that ISO 9000 is good for business

There has been no research to show that registration to ISO 9000 brings business benefits, and plenty to show otherwise. Recent research conducted by the Association of Chartered Certified Accountants[*] showed that there was no evidence to sup-

---

[*] Bowie, N. and Owen, H. (1996), "An Investigation into the Relationship between Quality Improvement and Financial Performance", Chartered Association of Certified Accountants.

port the view that ISO 9000 registered organisations perform better than non-registered organisations, and there is a possibility that ISO 9000 is costing more than companies realise.

We strongly recommend that you get this talked about amongst the managers and staff of your organisation. If you are not registered to ISO 9000 it should provide a healthy brake on going forward. If you are registered to ISO 9000, take a look at your own circumstances. What evidence can you find of sub-optimisation which is directly attributable to registration? When you do this, don't ask those who have been responsible for implementation. Follow the progress of customer demands through your system and talk to the people who do the work. The people responsible for ISO 9000 may be prepared to be open and join you in questioning what has been done, but they are more likely to seek to defend their actions (or blame others for not "doing as they should").

But What if I Have to Do ISO 9000?

Keep challenging the "have to". The most common reason for registration is that customers are demanding it. If you can show your customers that you understand what matters to them and you have translated their needs into the way you manage your business, why should you need the Standard? There is not a customer in the world who would not be persuaded by data showing evidence of your performance against what matters to them.

If you have done this and you still think you "have to", that your customers will accept nothing else, the first thing you should work on is selecting your assessor. You need a relationship with someone who is not going to spoil your business by insisting on irrelevant or over-bureaucratic work. Meet with many assessors. Interview them on their interpretation of the Standard as it applies to your organisation. Ask them for their views as to which features of the Standard can result in poor quality. Ask them about the weaknesses (as they see it) of the Standard and how they might be overcome in your case. Any assessor who claims there are no weaknesses should be struck off your list.

At the same time, work with your own people to understand how well your organisation works at the moment. Do not start by having people document what they currently do; start by looking at the organisation as a system and follow the principles discussed in chapters 4 and 6. Generally, when you first take a view of an organisation as a system you will find plenty of obvious things to correct. Make immediate changes to things which can be changed without damaging the overall system. Where more detailed investigation is required, take the time to find out what is happening predictably and why. Put aside registration to the Standard for the whole of this period. Consider, for your system, what (minimal) control you need for managing and improving the work, regardless of its apparent fit with the requirements of ISO 9000.

If you take these steps you should find that performance improves. You should not go forward with registration until you are certain you have the right means of control (measures) in the right places. When you start to think about documentation take the view that you will document only the minimum — how you achieve clarity of what people do and how people work with measures to control and improve what they do. Discuss what you propose to document with your assessor and listen to his response. Do everything you can to avoid creating extra work (doing work and then writing about it; independent inspection). Insist that all inspection is self-inspection or audits at the request of the people who have responsibility for operations. Find out what the assessor is going to agree to and satisfy yourself that what you will be expected to do is of overall value to the business. This is your last opportunity to find out if you are likely to have problems with your assessor before you sign him up.

Then hope you have chosen the right assessor. And above all, remember Oscar Wilde's words: "There is no sin except stupidity".

RECOMMENDED READING

Books

Davis, R. (1994), *Beyond The BS5750/ISO 9000 Certificate*; Stanley Thornes

Deming, W. (1988), *Out of the Crisis*; Massachusetts Institute of Technology, Centre for Advanced Engineering Study (1986); Cambridge: Cambridge University Press.

Deming, W. (1993), *The New Economics*; Massachusetts Institute of Technology, Centre for Advanced Engineering Study.

Neave, H. (1990), *The Deming Dimension*; Knoxville, TN: SPC Press.

Ohmae, K. (1990), *The Borderless World: Power and Strategy in the Interlinked Economy*, London: Harper Collins.

*Owen, M. (1993), *SPC and Business Improvement* Bedford, UK: IFS Ltd.

Seddon, J. (1992), *I Want You to Cheat: The Unreasonable Guide to Service and Quality in Organisations*, Buckingham, UK: Vanguard Press.

Senge, P. (1992), *The Fifth Discipline*, London: Century Business.

*Wheeler, D. and Chambers, D. (1986) *Understanding Statistical Process Control,* Knoxville, TN: SPC Press and New York: Addison-Wesley (1990).

Womack, J., Jones, D. and Roos, D. (1991), *The Machine That Changed The World*, New York: Harper Collins.

CD-ROM
*Seddon, J. (1996), "Change Management Thinking", Vanguard Multimedia, Buckingham, UK.

* These resources show you how to create control charts; the cd-rom includes software which calculates, draws and prints control charts.

INDEX

ABOUT THE AUTHOR

John Seddon is an occupational psychologist, researcher, lecturer and Managing Director of Vanguard Consulting. A leading authority on managing change in organisations, he is also the author of *I Want You to Cheat: The Unreasonable Guide to Service and Quality in Organisations* and has recently released a highly-acclaimed CD-ROM for managers entitled "Change Management Thinking" (see back pages for details). He can be contacted at:

Vanguard Consulting
Villiers House
1 Nelson Street
Buckingham MK18 1BU
Telephone: (01280) 822255
Fax: (01280) 822266
http://www.vanguardconsult.co.uk

There is a better way!

Change Management Thinking

The New CD-ROM from Vanguard Multimedia

This pathbreaking CD-ROM will help any company improve performance through better management development. More than just another management tool, this programme **will change the way managers think**. *Change Management Thinking*:

- Challenges current management wisdom

- Exposes reasons for failure of popular change programmes

- Shows how changing thinking about how to manage can produce **breakthrough** results.

As well as providing managers with the intellectual and practical support they need to break the mould of traditional thinking, the CD-ROM also introduces them to the concepts and tools derived from **systems thinking** — the most important subject for managers to understand in order to compete in the 21st century.

What Customers Are Saying:

"The best computer-based learning resource I have yet to come across. Its tone is hard-hitting, provocative and often inspiring." — Paul Matheson, Consultant, Strathclyde Regional Council.

"The quality of information in this package is second to none. It covers, and more, everything I have ever read on the subject of quality." — Dave Scarbow, Customer Services Division, IBM UK.

"This CD-ROM provides easy access to reference material, hints and exercises to stimulate management action, and a user-friendly way of introducing managers to the better way of thinking." — Chris Whitfield, Management Development Manager, Guardian Insurance, UK.

How to Order

✉ By mail — Post this order form with your cheque or credit card details for immediate dispatch.

▤ By fax — Fax order form with credit card details to 0181-892 8379 in the UK or to 01-676 1644 in Ireland.

☎ By phone — Telephone your order to 0181-892 8379 in the UK or to 01-676 1600 in Ireland.

🖳 By e-mail — E-mail your order to oaktreep@iol.ie.

Yes, I wish to:

❐ Order the CD-ROM (£495.00 plus £10.00 P+P in UK or Ireland)

❐ Arrange for a demonstration.

❐ Order a Sampler (£10.00 plus £1.00 P+P in UK or Ireland (will be credited against purchase of CD-ROM))

❐ Cheque enclosed for £_____

Please charge my ❐ Access ❐ Visa

_____ _____ _____
Credit card number   Exp date   Signature

Name _____

Title _____

Company _____

Address _____

_____

Telephone_____ Fax _____

Send order form to:

Oak Tree Press, 4 Alexandra Road,
Twickenham, Middlesex TW1 2HE
Telephone: 0181-892 8379. Fax: 0181-892 8379

or

Oak Tree Press, Merrion Building,
Lower Merrion Street, Dublin 2, Ireland
Telephone: 01-676 1600. Fax: 01- 676 1644